Connecting the Dots

Man, God, Angels, and Demons

Other books by Dave Shaw

Please visit your favorite online book/ebook retailer, to discover other books by Dave Shaw:

Connecting the Dots – Man, God, Angels, and Demons *is the first and foundational book of the Connecting the Dots series*

This will be followed in short order by
Connecting the Dots - The Face of God
Connecting the Dots - Creavolution
Connecting the Dots - Parables

Please visit Dave's website:
http://www.DaveShawAuthor.com

Man, God, Angels, and Demons

Satan's role in Christianity

A book in the series

Connecting the Dots

by

Dave Shaw

Copyright © 2015 Dave Shaw
Published by Dave Shaw

ISBN-13: 978-1512214093

ISBN-10: 1512214094

License Notes

All rights reserved under U.S. and International copyright law. This book may not be copied, scanned, digitally reproduced, or printed for re-sale, may not be uploaded on shareware or free sites, or used in any manner except the quoting of brief excerpts for the purpose of reviews, promotions, or articles without the express written permission of the author and/or publisher.

Cover Design by Laura Shinn Designs
http://laurashinn.yolasite.com

Copyright notice regarding Bible verses quoted in this book:

Scriptures taken from the Holy Bible, New International Version®, NIV®. Copyright © 1973, 1978, 1984, 2011 by Biblica, Inc.™ Used by permission of Zondervan. All rights reserved worldwide. http://zondervan.com The "NIV" and "New International Version" are trademarks registered in the United States Patent and Trademark Office by Biblica, Inc.™

Acknowledgments

Pastor Tom Longman. The year before writing this book, being unable to find a job in my chosen career, I became very despondent, to the point of giving up hope. I found hope again when Jesus pulled me back from a very dark place. I wrote a message that I wanted to give to our congregation. My church has many homeless people in the congregation, and I hoped it would give those who were in a dark place hope as well. In God's timing, and some months later, I tacked it onto one of Tom's sermons. I knew God wanted me to give that message; it was titled 'Hope'.

Jeff Simla heard that message and said I should be a writer; a few others backed up his statement and so began my new life as a writer.

Deb Galpin and **Loralea Vutikofer** read through the first rather badly structured version of this book. It is through their help and advice that I hope you will find this book full of revelation, but now not laid out like a technical document.

Linda Westberg graciously offered to edit my book for free. She is a professional editor and taught this old grammar schoolboy that he didn't remember as much as he thought he did.

Laura Shinn prepared the cover and formatted the ebook for submission to Smashwords and Amazon, and for CreateSpace for the paperback. It was a creative battle for me, a painter, but she is an electronic arts specialist and *she* had the brush!

Jo Shaw put up with me, while I was learning some of the finer points of Word. Even the dog tried to hide under the bed at times. Great thanks to my wife of 43 years for completing the last 5 ½ hours marathon in the early hours of the morning for the final proof read. I don't know if anyone makes as many mistakes as me, so please forgive the gleanings.

Review

"DAVE SHAW has some really good stuff here. He has a personable, pleasant non-condescending way of writing, in spite of the fact his topic is theology. He makes difficult topics attainable. And he has beautiful word-pictures. My favourite chapter is The Tapestry; it was gorgeous. I admire the way he brings the whole thing together over God using Satan (and all events) to polarize. I think this is fresh and new, and needs to be out there."
—*Loralea Vutikofer*

Cover Artwork Paintings

The top cover artwork is a cropped image of 'The creation of Adam', which was painted by Michelangelo on the ceiling of the Sistine chapel in 1512. The lower artwork is a montage of two old masters with some blending by Laura.

Table of Contents

Introduction	1
The First Dot	7
There was War in Heaven	21
Cast Down to Earth	41
There was War on Earth	57
The Battlefield	71
Psy-Ops	87
The Tapestry	99
Bookends	123
Assumptions	131
If I were God	137
Creating a Nation God's Way	143
God's Weather Forecast	203
Lucifer	219
Angel Society	229
The Banquet	237
My Testimony	245
About the Author	252

INTRODUCTION

This book is the first in a series *connecting the dots* that I see in the Bible to reveal more than the Bible's literal content. You could call it reading between the lines, but it is much more than that, it goes broader and deeper, linking many seemingly unrelated passages in the Bible. It is meant for non-Christians and Christians alike. For non-Christians, it may demonstrate that there is reason and order in the Bible, revealing a big picture of God's plan unfolding, and lead to a belief that God is real, and the Bible is less fable and more a vast archive about the nature of God Himself. For some Christians like me, it may answer some of the questions that, although not essential, may provide even more proof that God is in control, showing that some of the most baffling events are actually part of a very big plan, spanning much more than the time of mankind on earth.

Although I have written periodically since my youth, it was just heart stuff wanting to see the light. After almost 50 years in technology, mainly in design, and having studied the Bible for 25 years, my analytical mind wanted answers beyond what was simply stated in the Bible, or what I found written about elsewhere. For me it seemed there were many blanks in the Bible, either intentional or not. I'm sure all the essentials are in the Bible to fulfill God's plans for us as individuals, but if I have questions, I'm sure others do also.

In this series of books I use the innate skills I developed as a designer, to recognize patterns, make inferences, and overlay what logic I can to form a big picture regarding seemingly disconnected events and passages. What is written in the Bible, the statements or passages that leave me with a big question, I call *dots*. I try to offer a logical, but inferred connection, and these are the lines connecting the dots, the relationships between them.

I ponder things that don't sit right with me in the Bible, and usually, sooner or later there's a little flash that turns into a dim glow; the aha moment. As I focus on each issue that troubles me the glow brightens and that dot will connect to other dots, as my mind lets me know what it is seeing. The flash is the feeling that there is some type of link; the glow comes like fog lifting, revealing the nature of the link. That moment for this book came about four years ago, but I was deep in design for a large technology project, and I put the blurry image of connections off until I could research it further.

That initial aha moment has grown as one by one the dots have linked to each other to form the skeleton of an overall picture. This wasn't the result of conscious research, although that has since been a large part of this book, but instead it was something below my consciousness, chewing on the issues, forming concepts. The picture began to connect a carefully orchestrated sequence of events, not yet complete, but inferring the events had been planned.

Introduction

The aha moment said that there had to be some rational reasons why an all knowing God, who sees and knows everything in the past, present and future, would create the angel Lucifer, the angel of light, who would later become Satan the fallen angel of darkness (don't get bent out of my use of the name Lucifer, it is explained in the Chapter of that name). God knows everything, He *sees* the future. He knew Lucifer would become Satan. If you knew you would end up in a car crash, would you even start the journey? Knowing that this angel would one day lead a rebellion in heaven made no sense (to me). But while I was still perplexed, there was a flash, dots began to join and other dots appeared in the dim glow of a big picture, a very big picture.

I already understood it was God's plan to have exquisite fellowship with His creation; to love those He had created and to be loved in return, more and more, as the relationship developed. Besides being infinite in all abilities, God's essence is limitless love. As many people do, I found it hard to reconcile the evil in this world with a loving God. God is consumed with such a depth of love for His creation and to be reconciled to us, that He gave His only Son, Jesus, to satisfy His unavoidable justice that our dark thoughts and acts require. I believe this plan, for us to be reconciled with God, was formed long before the angels and the earth were created; if I am right it is a huge plan. As I researched, more and more elements fleshed out the dot picture, and I try to lay them out in a logical order for you to judge for yourself.

There is an underlying thread of love in the Bible starting in Genesis right through to Revelation. I believe that everything in the Bible is there for a reason, and maybe every single thing is woven into a vast tapestry, if I only I could see it. I know there are other dot pictures in the Bible that I can sense, and that is why I know that I will write more books in the series.

Over the centuries science has gradually stripped mankind of his garb of self-importance. Once, mankind was the centre of the universe, he and his dominion were majestic in the universe; in his own mind anyway. The earth and whoever considered themselves most important were at the centre of the universe. The rest of the universe was reduced to a cloth hung over our dominion spattered with tiny lights. We dressed the clusters of mighty star systems in simplistic pictures of not-so-perfect gods.

Science has revealed our more humble place in the cosmos, but not our place and relationship in the bigger view of God's realms. I hope this book starts to shed some light beyond our realm, and into the realms of the angels. I try to link events in the heavenly realms, one of which I believe is the realm of our earth. It seems to fit, just like the gaps in the early periodic table, hinted at undiscovered elements.

The relationship between our earth, which now is Satan's domain, and God's heaven would appear to be governed by rules, just as the cosmos has its equations of motion and gravity. Of course I do not leave out the subset of angels

Introduction

referred to as Fallen Angels or more commonly, as demons. No longer do I see Satan as just messing things up; he would seem to be a key element in God's plan.

I hope you find the ideas I propose in this book thought provoking. If you do not call yourself a Christian, I hope it prompts you to look further into your relationship with whatever you call or think of as God, even being as bold as to ask Him to reveal Himself to you personally. Or if you have started your journey with Jesus, I hope that this book gives you more confidence that your current walk with God is part of a greater plan. Growing a relationship in your world of circumstances, that often does not seem to make sense, is a carefully sewn thread in the great tapestry of God's plan. I hope this book allows you to see the big picture from God's perspective, and gives you confidence that He has billions of plans for individuals, as it is *we* who are the focus of this very big picture.

The former chapters are the meat, while the subsequent chapters go into much more detail about the reasoning and other observations I made while writing this book. If you are a Christian, some of the latter chapters may be a refresher, sprinkled with insights. If you are not already a Christian, it will provide some background into Christianity and will help put the earlier chapters in context.

Some of this book is quite deep and to lighten it up I have added little episodes of my life with my dog Jasmine and other perspectives called *Dog Days*.

Then the Lord said to Satan, "Have you considered my servant Job? There is no one on earth like him; he is blameless and upright, a man who fears God and shuns evil."

~ Job 1:8

THE FIRST DOT

I struggled to find words that would adequately describe the perception I first had about the ideas and concepts that have come to me. It gives me a measure of peace, about the 'whys' that wave flags at me from behind some phrases and statements in the Bible. I started to attend Bible studies just after I became a Christian and that really helped me to understand the ever important context. That little bit of help was all I needed to get hooked; I started to read the whole Bible, and completed it in a few months. It's like God scattered clues for a multidimensional crossword puzzle across the whole Bible. I encountered the first question, the first 'why', almost as soon as I began to read the Bible. I came across the book of Job. I was searching for God in the Bible. I had started at the beginning, learning the basics of the origins and development of the nation of the Hebrews, the forbears of the modern nation of Israel. I had many questions, but assumed I would find the answers later in the Bible, or when my understanding grew. It took me 20 years before I got most of the answers I was looking for.

Job is a good sized book and has many lessons for us. Chapter 1 left me with many more questions than answers. It is quite self-contained, not seeming to depend directly on other parts of the Bible; it is apparently much older than any other book in the Bible. It is a brief skeleton of a story about

God, Satan and a man, Job, who is kept in ignorance of why the events in his life were unfolding the way they were. It obviously took place before the crucifixion of Jesus, still in the time when Satan was recruiting his following and accusing men of their weak, if any, loyalty to God.

Job, Chapter 1

[1]In the land of Uz there lived a man whose name was Job. This man was blameless and upright; he feared God and shunned evil. [2]He had seven sons and three daughters, [3]and he owned seven thousand sheep, three thousand camels, five hundred yoke of oxen and five hundred donkeys, and had a large number of servants. He was the greatest man among all the people of the East.

[4]His sons used to hold feasts in their homes on their birthdays, and they would invite their three sisters to eat and drink with them. [5]When a period of feasting had run its course, Job would make arrangements for them to be purified. Early in the morning he would sacrifice a burnt offering for each of them, thinking, "Perhaps my children have sinned and cursed God in their hearts." This was Job's regular custom.

[6]One day the angels came to present themselves before the LORD, *and Satan also came with them. [7]The* LORD *said to Satan, "Where have you come from?"*

Satan answered the LORD, *"From roaming throughout the earth, going back and forth on it."*

The First Dot

⁸Then the LORD said to Satan, "Have you considered my servant Job? There is no one on earth like him; he is blameless and upright, a man who fears God and shuns evil."

⁹"Does Job fear God for nothing?" Satan replied. ¹⁰"Have you not put a hedge around him and his household and everything he has? You have blessed the work of his hands, so that his flocks and herds are spread throughout the land. ¹¹But now stretch out your hand and strike everything he has, and he will surely curse you to your face."

¹²The LORD said to Satan, "Very well, then, everything he has is in your power, but on the man himself do not lay a finger."

Then Satan went out from the presence of the LORD.

¹³One day when Job's sons and daughters were feasting and drinking wine at the oldest brother's house, ¹⁴a messenger came to Job and said, "The oxen were plowing and the donkeys were grazing nearby, ¹⁵and the Sabeans attacked and made off with them. They put the servants to the sword, and I am the only one who has escaped to tell you!"

¹⁶While he was still speaking, another messenger came and said, "The fire of God fell from the heavens and burned up the sheep and the servants, and I am the only one who has escaped to tell you!"

¹⁷While he was still speaking, another messenger came and said, "The Chaldeans formed three raiding parties and swept down on your camels and made off with them. They put the

servants to the sword, and I am the only one who has escaped to tell you!"

¹⁸While he was still speaking, yet another messenger came and said, "Your sons and daughters were feasting and drinking wine at the oldest brother's house, ¹⁹when suddenly a mighty windswept in from the desert and struck the four corners of the house. It collapsed on them and they are dead, and I am the only one who has escaped to tell you!"

²⁰At this, Job got up and tore his robe and shaved his head. Then he fell to the ground in worship ²¹and said:

"Naked I came from my mother's womb, and naked I will depart. The LORD gave and the LORD has taken away; may the name of the LORD be praised."

²²In all this, Job did not sin by charging God with wrongdoing.

It is a happy ever after story and in the end, after many lessons, Job gets twice as much as he had before and a new family, after initially losing all he had including all his children. If I were him though, I'm sure I would have preferred for God to do whatever He was up to with Satan another way. But Job a true servant of God, took it all in stride, even if he did demand an explanation; which he never did get.

Now bearing in mind that this is way before Jesus came to earth and His work of salvation; it would be when, and the

Bible itself verifies, Satan was 'debating' with God about the verity of man's love for God. Satan must have been a bit confused why God was still working in this way, as if Satan had not corrupted mankind back at the dawn of his existence, creating an unbridgeable chasm to prevent mankind ever being resurrected and living in the presence of God. It was true; the nation of Israel had demonstrated effectively that they could not keep God's laws to justify their entrance into God's heaven. This is widely held to be God's way of showing mankind just how powerless he was to be holy in his own strength.

There are two threads going on here in the first Chapter. First the context and life of Job and his family, and secondly is the conversation between God and Satan. This Chapter raises so many questions for me starting in verse 6, bearing in mind Satan had already corrupted man.

Why was Satan tagging along with the angels? Obviously this was before he had been banished, cast down to earth. God strikes up a seemingly casual conversation, "Where have you been?" As if God did not know, "same old, same old" replies Satan. This is strange, Satan had corrupted man, determined to thwart God's plan for mankind before it even gets going, but God invites him into a conversation. This is the period after man's corruption and before Satan and his followers are kicked out of God's heaven. We don't know if, at this point, Satan has a following or if it's just between him and God. But it is clear that God is fostering the 'debate' about His authority, and more importantly the love bond He is establishing with men. It was likely to have been a gradual affair, as Satan and his followers become emboldened; demons were certainly active when Jesus was on earth as He spent some considerable time casting them out of people, and the Bible devotes many stories to this act in various forms. God was obviously fully aware that Satan had corrupted His latest creation from the beginning. Did He call Satan to stand before Him and give an account? We are never told, but God is patient and has a plan, a plan that includes Satan! Was Satan emboldened by pulling off his corruption stunt and not being immediately zapped by God? Would God's justice allow Him to do that? I think God knew exactly what Satan was up to and was playing along, or rather playing him; for God, this phase of His plan had only just started.

Back to Satan in the presence of God - God initiates a challenge with "Look at Job; what a great guy, honest and obedient. He honours me in all things." This probably pressed a few of Satan's buttons that would send him off on a tirade about how it's just because God blesses Job so much. So God sets Satan loose on Job, but Job does not turn from God. The scenario almost repeats itself in the next Chapter, where Job has nothing but his health left.

Job Chapter 2

[1] On another day the angels came to present themselves before the LORD, and Satan also came with them to present himself before him. [2] And the LORD said to Satan, "Where have you come from?"

Satan answered the LORD, *"From roaming throughout the earth, going back and forth on it."*

³Then the LORD said to Satan, "Have you considered my servant Job? There is no one on earth like him; he is blameless and upright, a man who fears God and shuns evil. And he still maintains his integrity, though you incited me against him to ruin him without any reason."

⁴"Skin for skin!" Satan replied. "A man will give all he has for his own life. ⁵But now stretch out your hand and strike his flesh and bones, and he will surely curse you to your face."

⁶The LORD said to Satan, "Very well, then, he is in your hands; but you must spare his life."

⁷So Satan went out from the presence of the LORD and afflicted Job with painful sores from the soles of his feet to the crown of his head. ⁸Then Job took a piece of broken pottery and scraped himself with it as he sat among the ashes.

⁹His wife said to him, "Are you still maintaining your integrity? Curse God and die!"

¹⁰He replied, "You are talking like a foolish woman. Shall we accept good from God, and not trouble?"

In all this, Job did not sin in what he said.

A number of questions scream out to me from just the first two Chapters, but only one really had me stumped. Why did God provoke Satan to attack Job? Notice that Satan returned after the first bout of torment meted out to Job, but after he had done everything he was allowed to do, short of killing Job, he did not argue his case any longer, in this story anyway.

Job seemed to be God's ideal guy, a real child of God. The book later goes on to teach many great lessons about how we judge and put our intellect on a level with God's. God proceeds to put us in our place, through Job. Throughout the trials Job was never told why it all happened, although initially he demanded to know why. By the end of the book, family and wealth are restored to Job, even more than he had before, but it does not answer why it all happened in the first place. From my earliest days as a Christian I have felt *Job'd*. Those times when, although we are walking upright (or as much as we are able), one thing after another starts to fall apart. It is in times like these that God seems to be letting us see where our relationship stands with Him. Just because we think we have an unbreakable faith, we don't really know until it's tested. It's just like testing metal that comes from a furnace; it isn't assumed it has the correct strength. It is tested and pulled apart until it breaks. For me it has been God's stress test; letting me see my progress, and how far I still have to go on my journey. Satan must have had a field day 'testing' mankind, but God, besides feeling the hurt of His children, must have been glad at the progress He saw. Once it went on with God's permission; now it takes place within the constraints God has placed on Satan and his demons.

I think this story of Job is representative of many stories that could be recounted in Old Testament times (times before Jesus' crucifixion). Although many Christians believe it is happening to them in the present day, as did I, I think it is a different type of interaction we have with Satan now. Satan is clearly on this earth, as he had been by the command of God from at least the dawn of man; the angels' job was to *minister* to man. But after the war in heaven, which was demarked by the salvation work of Jesus, the debate with Satan and his accusations against man, as in the story of Job, ended. They were cast out of heaven, and limited to the other domains outside God's heaven. Even though it may seem the same to us; now Satan is completely his own agent, just operating within the limits God has placed on the fallen angels' powers. There are still twice as many of God's faithful angels as there are fallen angels. God's angels have access to us, in our realm, and the fallen angels' realm, keeping them in check.

I think the power Satan has over mankind is now radically different. God gave Satan free will over how to inflict devastation on Job, within limits, as long as he didn't kill him. In this, Job was a pawn, used as an empirical study over whether he truly honoured God, for who He was, regardless of His blessings; for us it is a generic example. Now I think God is still using Satan as a polarizing agent, not in heaven, that time is over, but now on earth. Even though God set boundaries on Satan and his demons' works, they seem to be operating more with a mandate of vengeance against God;

although at times it seems hard to distinguish between vengeance against us, and vengeance against God. I think we are just collateral damage in Satan's rage against God because he is powerless against God himself, and angels can defend themselves.

The dialogue with Satan is not the essence of this book but it is a clear instance where there are really bizarre events, (from our perspective), that are stated in a very clear way, and raise obvious questions of just plain WHY? Over the years I have had more and more questions.

We know a lot more about earth than the other heavens. We literally see our earth, but we seem to accept various, vague, and often half myth ideas about heaven. It seems we reference heaven in this world, but the mainstream has left the true descriptions of heaven in the Bible. We don't seem to be able to wrap our heads around it, or don't want to.

So here we have Satan cast down to earth, but largely invisible to us, so this may be another heaven, A third of all the angels, the ones who sided with Satan, are also cast down from God's heaven to earth with Satan, who are widely referred to as Satan's demons.

So imagine, if you will, our earth sitting in our cosmos, the first heaven, with a parallel dimension we cannot enter or see. That dimension is the realm of the second heaven. The second heaven, envelops the earth, and extends to the third heaven. Satan and his demons are relegated to the first and second heavens, their realm and the earth as it is a parallel dimension. Satan is referred to as the prince of the air, and he roams the earth, seeking to devour men. The third heaven is God's heaven, where He resides and is attended by His angels. God's angels seem to have free roam of all the heavens, while Satan and his demons, since they were *cast down to earth*, are restricted to the first and second combination, with very limited, or no access to God's heaven to converse with God. I think conversations, such as that in Job ended when Satan and his angels were *cast down to earth*. We are of course limited to the first heaven, the cosmos, bound by time and physical matter. There are exceptions to this, as many times according the Bible some men have gone to the third heaven.

God's angels have been manifest on earth, looking like regular humans. According to Howard Pitman, (see an explanation of his out of body experience in the Chapter *There was War in Heaven*), there are more demons than men on the earth. All the angels and demons can see us, but we only see what's in the first heaven, our cosmos. It would seem there are billions of angels, some faithful to God others now demons and excluded from God's heaven. Are these billions of angels and demons just milling around, waiting to be given a job by God or Satan? The Bible does not shed a clear light on this, but does mention some of the roles that God's angels have: for example the angels who watch over children, messengers, angels performing tasks, such as the destruction of Sodom and Gomorrah, to say nothing of the devastation they wreak in the tribulation.

What did Satan do before he rebelled against God? Satan and all the demons were initially created by God, presumably for His pleasure. The Bible says we were created slightly below the angels, so they are *humans+*, and we were created in His image. I think the main elements about being created in His image are that we have free will, that we are creative, and that we have the capacity for love. The angels certainly have greater power than us, it seems every time a human encounters one they end up on their face quaking, and the angel has to reassure the human, not to be afraid. At other times they are not so intimidating and we see them in human form. Pitman makes an observation, which ties in with the demons being so set against humans, especially those close to Jesus. He says they seem focused on their purpose, in a way that would make any army commander proud.

The First Dot

 Dog Days

I started this book four years ago, but it died a death by the distraction of technology and business. Jumbug, my Great Dane, would commandeer two seats of the three seat sofa, where I sat with my remote keyboard, using the large flat screen TV as a monitor. It was a relaxing place to ponder, looking out to the west side of the Okanagan valley's 84 mile (135 km) long lake. When they are not asleep, Great Danes demand a lot of attention; they are clever, but a little brain is a dangerous thing, and a big nose can press five keys at once. Their body uses two seats of a sofa, and their ten pound head only temporarily resists the opportunity to rest on the third seat; whether it is occupied or not.

Now, it's almost four years to the day, in another house, looking out to the east side of the lake. Jumbug, my Great Dane, has passed on, and her role as companion has not quite been taken over by a Golden Doodle. Jasmine is either quite stupid or is able to hide her vast intellect with the subtleness of the 80 pound sheep that she resembles. We keep her eyelashes trimmed to about an inch, and have to brush her curly locks up over her eyes to look and see if anyone's home, but there never is. She has been an integral part of this book, as she reminds me periodically it's time for a rub-arama, something I'll explain later. This has kept my eyes from developing a fixed focal length, and stopped too much blood pooling in my butt and legs; she's my green tea time alarm.

I know a man in Christ who fourteen years ago was caught up to the third heaven. Whether it was in the body or out of the body I do not know--God knows.

~ 2 Corinthians 12:2

THERE WAS WAR IN HEAVEN

In this Chapter, we will work through the inferences of the profound single first sentence in Revelation Chapter 12, verse 7, that I believe is at the root of many of our misunderstandings about the evil we see and experience on this earth.

Revelation Chapter 12

[7]Then war broke out in heaven. Michael and his angels fought against the dragon, and the dragon and his angels fought back. [8]But he was not strong enough, and they lost their place in heaven. [9]The great dragon was hurled down— that ancient serpent called the devil, or Satan, who leads the whole world astray. He was hurled to the earth, and his angels with him.

This passage is brief but the events are central to a plan that had a definite sequence. The very first sentence infers volumes. How do you get to the point of war, can you work backwards? I believe so. Immediately before the war you need to have a disagreement. Because of pride Satan grew to resent God and aspired to lift himself above the angels and even be 'like' God. However he was only an angel; albeit beautiful, wise, powerful, and blameless in all his ways.

Angels are not stupid, from their vantage point in heaven much of what is going on is obvious to them, whereas our perception is veiled. Even with Satan's deception, lies, and possible promises of higher positions and freedom under his rule, an angel would have to be quite willful to go against, rebel against, Almighty God. What were they thinking! Our most accomplished politicians, skillful in their arts of fake humility, charisma, and persuasion, have nothing on Satan; he blows them away, as demonstrated by the billions led astray in heaven and on this earth. Imagine the persuasive power of Satan if he could cause billions of angels, who could see God and understood His power, to directly oppose God and think they could win. How deluded of God's Resolve and Majesty they were; and how vulnerable we are in our little lives that barely reach beyond the end of our noses.

The Bible refers to an archangel, Michael, who is in charge of the armies of God. Are all God's angels in His army, or does He have warring angels? It would seem strange to be in a society where there is a large army, but no enemy; I am talking about the time before the earth. It seems Satan was at Michael's level, but Michael wields more authority, God's authority. When was Michael created, just before the war, or long, long before? Did he need credentials, a track record, before being assigned to the status of archangel, in charge of the armies of God? Why would God create a 'warring' angel, why did He have armies? It seems unlikely He would create Michael at the onset of war in a reactionary manner, He doesn't act like that, and with good reason; He can see the future and never gets in that predicament. Like Satan, Michael was most likely created long before the war in heaven, even if he and the other eventual 'soldiers' in God's armies, were not overtly viewed as warriors initially, God must have planned for that. Whether they understood it at the beginning of their unrest with the status quo, or at the time war broke out in heaven, those who sided with Satan, were in Satan's army, marked for ever as rebels against God's rule, God's way. According to Pitman there are fallen angels who are so scary that even the other demons steer clear of them.

There are only two references in the Bible regarding Michael. One in Jude where it says Michael, when disputing over the body of Moses did not dare to condemn or slander Satan, but merely said "The Lord rebuke you." Is this a level of decorum with which war is waged in heaven; a level we rarely witness on earth? It's like the pomp at the surrender of the Japanese forces in the Second World War. Do all angels have strict limitations on their authority and power? The other time Michael is mentioned is in a vision of Daniel, as Daniel relates starting in the book of Daniel Chapter 10. In this vision, the angel, who was giving Daniel the meaning of a message Daniel had received from God, explained that he had been delayed three weeks by the *prince of Persia*, Satan, until Michael came to help him. Maybe that was a question of authority as well. There seems to be defined limits to angel's authority; this is clearly demonstrated in the story of Job.

Presumably Michael is one of many powerful warring angels, and presumably there are warring angels on the side of the rebels also. I have often pondered how angels make war. They are spirits and wage war in Heaven. From what the Bible says, it seems it is more of a question of authority. I do not believe there is matter, physical stuff as we know it, in heaven; it would not be a lot of use to spirits. I imagine the closest spirits come to trying to wage spiritual war is two puffs of vapour bumping chests; obviously not the way it is. Also I don't think constraint, as in *being delayed by the prince of Persia for three weeks*, is a very war like action. The word 'war' must somehow be fully justified. Descriptions of guardian cherubim flashing mighty swords to prevent Adam and Eve from re-entering the Garden of Eden to eat from the Tree of Life, sounds like they have a very serious side to them, besides ministering to us feeble humans. Cast down to earth, like an almighty lightning bolt from heaven, doesn't sound so gentle either. There is some violent action described as emanating from heaven, for example consuming fire on Sodom and Gomorrah, and the armies who confront Jesus in the final battle.

Despite the earth being an ideal place to wage a very physical and bloody war, I think Satan and his cohorts have a great deal to answer for in the bloody history of our earth, but I think the most likely arena for war in heaven and on earth would seem to be an intellectual one, although the finality takes a long time to realize. It seems there must have been debate and then war in heaven, maybe only debate as long as it served God's purposes. Then the war may have been merely a matter of the one third of the billions of angels being evicted from heaven by the other two thirds with the sheer authority of God's truth; here I can see the wielding of the *sword of God's Word*.

What was the core of Satan's argument to convince billions of angels to side with him in what must have started out to be a debate against God's premise that as angels and mankind we obey Him out of love? Does God need a reason, beyond that He created us for us to love and obey Him; it is not as if it is onerous, it's not *Metropolis* lived out. The vast majority of us, those who have not been lifted up to God's heaven and been *with* Him, have no idea of the Majesty that would, by its sheer greatness, compel us to fall on our faces. Mankind was created in the image of God. I suspect angels were also created in God's image, and as such they would be able to exercise free will and be capable of love. *Created in the image of God* is probably worthy of a book in itself, and would probably be very similar to my next book *The Face of God*.

As we see so readily on this earth there are two basic ways that love is manifested; outwardly and inwardly. Narcissism, the overpowering love of oneself, is the crest on the flag atop the castle built of pride, greed, arrogance, and all the other character ailments that destroy instead of build relationships. All the stones to build that castle reside in all of us, but they have to be quarried. Circumstances can provide tools for that work, but I think, in large part, the work order is signed by us, as more a conscious than an unconscious choice. God's commandments tell us to love Him with all that we are, and to love others, as we love ourselves. The latter part definitely applies a governing factor on how much we love ourselves, and uses the word love in an entirely different way than in a song that says "I'm too sexy for my shirt."

For some angels, even though they must have encountered God's Majesty, and sensed His Love in an unmistakable way, the choice to entertain thoughts of an existence, other than as God's servants, belied their lack of true love for their Creator. So the constituent sides were drawn up for the great debate, the prelude to the great war in heaven. As an intellectual war, the arguments being waged by both sides would have ultimately been about the authority of God and validity of Jesus. It is hard for me to contemplate how an angel, who has experienced God in a physical way, in His heaven, could even entertain ideas of going his own way, and doing his own thing. I would imagine their *physical* realm to be so much more engaging than our *physical* realm. I have to believe Jesus, who said and I paraphrase "you cannot imagine the wondrous paradise that is heaven." And it seems no one who saw it could explain it to us in words that gave it justice.

Even though no clear timeline is provided by the Bible, this must have all started when there was opportunity for God to establish relationship with man; the time of Adam and Eve, and of Lucifer transforming to Satan, when God created mankind with intelligence, at the dawn of Homo Sapiens, mankind who thinks. It is very unlikely that Satan would subvert the angels before this as he had it so good; *he was blameless in all his ways.*

Before this subversion, the heavens were populated by any number of types of heavenly beings, fully aware that they were created by God, by the design of the Father and made manifest by Jesus. In their sight they witnessed the creation of the cosmos, with the earth populated by mankind, in the image of God; obvious competitors for the attention of their Creator. By Satan *spinning* God's plan of love, mankind became the catalyst for dissention in the angel's heaven, and subsequently the fallen angels became the catalyst for man's dissention against God on earth. At a critical time, when the time was ripe, God ejected Satan and the other dissenters, rebels, from heaven, to continue the role He had for them on earth.

Satan seems to have a hard time accepting Jesus for who He is, resenting the worship by those who have been given to Him by the Father; all men who accept what He did for them on the cross, and desire to live with God after mortal death. Satan's premise, as our accuser (to God), is that our demonstration of that love is insincere, and is based on a natural reaction to the blessings God bestows on us. It seems that Satan thinks that Jesus has *stolen* his reward, and that he is worthy and deserving of the praise and worship of man, (and possibly angels). This almost smacks of Jacob *stealing* Esau's birthright and blessing from Abraham; he must have felt he deserved it more than Esau.

I think this was the prime motivator to all Satan's actions from day one; day one being when he was assigned to guard the Tree of the Knowledge of Good and Evil in the Garden of Eden. Instead of serving man, he wanted to be worshipped by these creatures that were created *just lower than the angels*. The war in heaven was a war of philosophies, but it was a smokescreen for what Satan was really after; recognition, a subplot of lived out pride.

As Lucifer, he may have been the ultimate angel, the apex in power, beauty, and intellect. But did God leave a crucial element out? Did he need love to be loyal in the times before man? He must have had the respect of all the other angels, and was likely honored by God for his service, and while he had these his lack of love for anyone except himself probably did not manifest any rebellious tendencies. It may have seemed that Jesus was being favoured unfairly, when the Father had Jesus create mankind and the cosmos, with a plan to have mankind serve and glorify Him. Lucifer considered himself almost equal to Jesus. Avoiding the fact that he did not have the creative power of Jesus, this was a minor issue in Lucifer's mind, and he must have thought that he rightly deserved to rule mankind for *his* pleasure. He thought he could scuttle this plan by corrupting man. He must have been confused and enraged by Jesus showing up in person, in the form of a human without his Godly powers.

Not being able to deduce God's *upside down* plan of having Jesus come to man's rescue after he had corrupted man, he frantically tried to prevent Jesus from being born and being effective in His ministry by trying to kill Him a number of times. Eventually he succeeded at the cross. By gross manipulation of the religious rulers, the mob, and even Pilate the Roman prefect of Judea, Satan succeeded in killing the human Jesus. However he totally failed to understand God's plan until it was too late; Jesus-human, was Jesus-God, He was perfect, and although he was *killed*, it was a sacrifice. It was Jesus' very death, Jesus' voluntary sacrifice that undid the work that Satan had done in the Garden of Eden. It was a death like no other man's death; completely sinless Jesus had placed on Him at that moment, all the sins of the world up to that point and from that point to the end of the earth. He received the penalty for them, which was separation from God the Father.

That is why Jesus called out at that moment;

"Eli, Eli, lama sabachthani which means "My God, my God, why have you forsaken me?".

Although Jesus prayed for *the cup to be taken from Him*, it would seem that Jesus was not expecting separation from the Father. Maybe the Father had not gone through His full plan in detail with Jesus-Human, and blocked the ramifications of Jesus-God; He had given up His power when He was born. The Father at that moment when Jesus was on the cross, placed the sins of the world on Jesus, just as the Jewish high priest placed the sins of the Jews on the scapegoat once a year, for the atonement of their sins. Having done that, and Jesus having become the ultimate sin burden in God's sight, the Father had to separate Himself from Jesus for the first time in eternity. The act of God placing the sins on Jesus, and Jesus atoning for all the sins of man, was an instantaneous affair, and took Satan by complete surprise. But Jesus, having paid the penalty, could not remain separated as He was inherently perfect. The penalty was paid, God's Justice satisfied, and there was now no chasm between mankind and God, for those who believed in what Jesus had done. No wonder Satan was as mad as hell, beyond resenting his lack of recognition, his plan had been thwarted and he was unceremoniously tossed out of heaven; he was visibly in every respect a *second class angel!*

It was also a milestone event. Up to that point it seems that Satan was accusing mankind before God, presumably in God's heaven, pleading his philosophical case. The angels seem to have had access to earth all the time as ministering angels, then as maybe partially obedient but dissenting angels, or fully dissenting angels, responding to what may have appeared to be an impotent God. But now the time for debate was over and they were banished from God's heaven and relegated to earth as demons. So much happened at the point of the atonement, when Jesus declared *"It is finished"* that realization must have literally stunned Satan, and as he comprehended the enormity, and finality of the event, he went into a rage. His tantrum has lasted for 2,000 years, and continues as he *roams the earth to see who he can devour.*

At this point, Satan and all his angels must have realized how big a mistake they had made. They had already been judged and they were banished from heaven; they were in the holding cells of earth and the second heaven, just waiting for God to carry out the sentence. For them all hope of reasoning with God was lost. God was not through with them. Just as He seems to use people who will never bend the knee to Him, like the Pharaoh of Egypt, He had thousands of years of work planned for them.

It seems many things occurred when they were *cast down to earth.* Some angels seemed to have been chained up in the bottomless pit; Satan's residence for a thousand years when the war on earth is over, before ending up himself in the lake of fire. The rest of the fallen angels are transformed into demons. Every last remnant of love and compassion seems to have been taken from them, and they are left with an illogical hatred for man; what had we done to them? It would seem that along with the various classes of angels there must have been various powers or attributes according to those classes. The angels who were chained in the bottomless pit must have had attributes too destructive to be released on the earth for a long period. The leading demon in the pit is called the *Destroyer.* Maybe they were of the warrior class and were fighting against God's army of angels, led by Michael, when the debate escalated into *war in heaven.* It seems this pit could also be the home of demons when they are not on a mission making someone's life more of a hell than it already is. When Jesus was casting out the demons, that identified themselves as 'Legion', from the man they had made insane, they asked to be sent into the nearby herd of pigs rather than being sent back to the *abyss*, most likely a reference to the bottomless pit. It is not just a pit. In the final days it is opened and the angels, who are chained there, will be released. It is said the smoke from the pit will block out the sun. Obviously it is a very nasty place, even if you do not have skin to burn or need air to breathe.

We need to have context for all this. It is hard to imagine these multi-dimensional places and their relationship to one another, but it seems that the earth and God's heaven are not that far from each other. Paul refers to a third heaven in his second letter to the Corinthians.

2 Corinthians Chapter 12

[2] *I know a man in Christ who fourteen years ago was caught up to the third heaven. Whether it was in the body or out of the body I do not know—God knows.*

What a strange thing to include in his letter without expanding upon it; definitely shouts a dot to me. I think the man Paul is referring to is himself. It is generally accepted that the first heaven is the earth, and there are some who say the second heaven is the cosmos. They look up to the sky when referring to God, but why separate earth and the cosmos; it is all governed by the same laws. Who inhabits that space? Would demons commute from earth where they tempt us, to meet, report, and plan on another planet or constellation, does God hold court in some galaxy far, far away?

In the Bible there is mention of *the pit* and imprisoning in *the lowest parts of the earth*, and *the abyss*. Some think that this is likely the place where the *sons of God*, who some speculate were angels who had sexual relations with the *daughters of men,* have been imprisoned *in chains* since the flood. Surely God placed controls on the form that angels, who manifested themselves as men of flesh on the earth, could take. When taking a fleshly form they were supposed to be on ministering errands for God so I do not imagine that He would allow them to even have genitals. Spirits do not have sexual relations, and neither will we in heaven, even with glorified bodies.

There is mention of angels leaving their proper place and being imprisoned. There is also mention that there were *angels* that Jesus preached to before ascending after His crucifixion. The word translated to *angels* here also has the meaning of *mankind* in the original language. The word has no other adjective asserting the translation to *angel*. This portion of text is more likely to refer to the Holy Spirit preaching repentance to men in the time of Noah. Any notion that any angels, who either *deserted their rightful domain*, or were kicked out of heaven, had any chance of re-entry into heaven is unsupported anywhere; why preach to them? It is also very weak speculation to say that these *angels*, if indeed they were angels at all, are the angels in the bottomless pit. A side note here is that the verse of Revelation 9:4 refers to *only those who did not bear the seal of God on their forehead*, inferring that there are those that did bear the seal of God;

saints, that is believers, were sealed in the period at the end of the tribulation.

A raging Satan is now roaming to and fro on the earth, listening, hearing our thoughts and prayers, seeing how he can strike the biggest blow against God. He has also read Revelation; he knows how it will end. He doesn't need to bother with those who he has already lured away from God's truth, or obedience to God, with the tinsel of this world, into a materialistic life style. He's after those who are seeking Jesus, and those who are leading them, those who have found Jesus, and those who disciple others. Angels don't sleep, God's angels nor fallen angels, why leave earth. They don't have to if they roam around in their element of a heavenly realm, like God's heaven, but outside, devoid of His light; a heaven that is outside God's heaven, but envelopes the earth. An understanding of the three heavens is not materially relevant to us seeking Jesus and salvation, but it does help us answer questions posed by statements in the Bible, and gives us visualization of the easy access demons have to us.

Howard Pitman, a Baptist minister for 35 years, had a near death experience and pleaded with the angel who came to him when he died on the operating table, to take him to present his case to God as to why he should live a while longer. He recalls his fascinating experience and description of the physical dimension and limitations of the beings in the first heaven (earth), the second heaven (a place for spirits, coexisting with earth and reaching to) the third heaven (the heaven of God). You can find his recollection of his near death experience at

https://www.youtube.com/watch?v=HasGkLsQ5gc

His recollection is full of detail, and even if you can't agree with what he saw, it does provide a good model to hang the arguments in this book on.

Howard Pitman describes a wide range of fallen angels, demons, and a *warrior class* that was feared and avoided by all the other demons. His description of this warring class is vivid and scary, and somehow capable of something more violent, but in spiritual ways, than even war on earth. In Gods heavenly realm, angels are spirits, they are not destroyed and do not die the way humans die. Our spirit does not die either at our mortal death. The rebelling angels were thrown out of God's heaven to earth. But in the Bible Satan is also called *prince of the air*. This passage from Ephesians Chapter 2 reveals another aspect of Satan being thrown to earth, and would seem to support Howard Pitman's description of the heavenly realms.

Ephesians Chapter 2

¹As for you, you were dead in your transgressions and sins, ²in which you used to live when you followed the ways of this world and of the ruler of the kingdom of the air, the spirit who is now at work in those who are disobedient.

The reference to mankind being *dead in his transgressions* refers to the fact we are already corrupted. We will always be separated from God, regardless of mortal death, unless we take advantage of the salvation mechanism offered by Jesus' sacrifice. Taking advantage of this salvation, we acquire God's Spirit and become joint heirs with Jesus in God's kingdom, whatever form that takes.

The Bible is sparse on the details about the war in heaven. The essence here though is the overt declaration of all the angels who made war against God, regardless of Satan's lies to them. They were judged and separated from God's presence. God is nothing if not just. He needs evidence. He is bound by His own justice. Even though He could have determined who was loyal to Him and His philosophy of absolute but just rule, was not the 100% evidence of their actions obvious to all? By default they were 'with God', God needed them to show by their actions, they were not. Satan sowed the seeds of sedition that must have sparked intense debate. At some point the sides were drawn up, and no one was left in the closet. Through some stages, whether it's debate, accusing and testing of 'men', such as in the story of Job, or through some form of violent confrontation, it was clear that Satan's side could not continue to cohabit God's heaven with the loyal angels. So Satan and his hoards were kicked out, cast 'down' to earth for the next stage in God's plan. I still wonder if the demarcation was strict. If you made war you were kicked out, but if you just attended the *sedition* rallies were you OK? Is there a repentance time for angels like people who are saved by the skin of their teeth, or does the Grace of God also cover angels who finally fight on God's side? I think God likes definitive action, in the same way that a woman can't be a little bit pregnant. Or then again, is it all in the heart; King David was called a man after God's own heart but he took Uriah's wife then had him killed? In God's court there will be no arguing. There will no pleading as in:

Matthew Chapter 7

²¹ "Not everyone who says to me, 'Lord, Lord,' will enter the kingdom of heaven, but only the one who does the will of my Father who is in heaven. ²²Many will say to me on that day, 'Lord, Lord, did we not prophesy in your name and in your name drive out demons and in your name perform many miracles?' ²³Then I will tell them plainly, 'I never knew you. Away from me, you evildoers!'

Yes I believe it is actions, but actions that stem from the heart. The book of James elaborates on this idea very well. I think in God's court, He will present the evidence and there will be no choice but to accept the verdict without arguing.

Dog Days

Jasmine is the dog I've always wanted; on the outside. She is an 80lb Golden Doodle, quite similar in appearance and intelligence to a sheep. She does not shed, and loves to cuddle. She has white curly hair with peachy patches on her knees and ears, and dark brown eyes; she looks so cute. It's probably the breed, but she has an insatiable appetite that causes her to steal whatever she can eat if she is left alone with food. I don't know whether it's her appetite but she feels the need to escape the yard. I think this because she raids the garbage bags and cans all over the neighbourhood when she escapes, and only comes back at the offer of her favourite large dog biscuits, and even then it seems only after she has completed her mine sweep. She is a bit of a tub, but still manages a Houdini and wriggles her way through the horizontal 2 by 4's that comprise the wood part of the fence; the 2 x 4's have eight inch gaps. Did I mention she is a bit of a tub, and she can barely get her head through the fence sideways? She must have some octopus genes for that is what she resembles doing her magic act. We keep her on a rope when we let her out but she still manages to rush off sometimes before we get her 'hooked up'. She either stubbornly refuses to obey, or just wants to do whatever she wants. What she lacks in intellect she makes up for in stubbornness.

Faced with this situation, and frustrated at the effort to dog proof the yard, I prayed. I prayed, "God, help me fix the dog." Instantly He replied, "You are like the dog..." We both went silent.

They were told not to harm the grass of the earth or any plant or tree, but only those people who did not have the seal of God on their foreheads.

~ Revelation 9:4

Cast Down to Earth

So having been convinced by Satan that God was unjust in His authoritarian rule, and presumably that they would have more fun under his rule, or even no rule at all, the less than fully loyal angels, joined the debate, but this was just the baby steps of their rebellion against God. Was this a surprise to God, a mistake that He needed to correct? No, of course not; it was God's plan, just one of the many steps to refine His creation. It seems to be a natural outcome of freewill, amongst angels and men. All it took was a catalyst, Lucifer, and possibly us, held up as a pawn for His reasoning. Many may have felt like Lucifer, that it was one thing to serve God, but quite another to minister to, or serve, humans. God knew that given the right conditions Lucifer would crack, revealing a truth that is even applicable in our world; power corrupts.

This is true of all of the man-created gods. They all have a mean streak, seeming to default to squashing us bugs; we have overlaid our nature upon them. Only God is perfect, pure, Holy, full of love, but equally full of justice, even being constrained by His Holy Laws. Jesus deferred to only God the Father as being perfect, when He was approached by a man calling Him "Good teacher." I think as the man referred to Him as teacher, not Messiah, or any reference to being God, I must assume Jesus was responding as if He was merely a man, human.

But now we are at a stage when all disloyal angels are readily identifiable. God's authority was publically questioned, and Satan had accomplished the task for which God had created him and played him for millennia. God had not been seriously entertaining their questions of His authority, but merely playing along so that all angels would show their true colours. Now the rebels were cast out of God's heaven, reducing their domain to the second heaven, and earth, the first heaven. This event was not singular; it was one of the events that cascaded from the Crucifixion of Jesus. Jesus had paid the penalty for man's sins once and for all; all sins past and in the future and God's Justice was satisfied. This was a surprise to Satan because God only placed the sins of mankind on Jesus at the last moment, but at that point it was too late and he had no remedy to prevent God the Father undoing the corruption of mankind in the Garden of Eden at the dawn of mankind.

Satan had created a wedge, a chasm, when he corrupted mankind in the Garden of Eden which neither mankind nor God could cross (because He is Holy and Just). Was Satan jealous that mankind was loved by God who desired a relationship with him; or was he jealous of the love that mankind had for Jesus and God the Father? I think it was more of the latter, and the fact that God wanted mankind to *dwell* with Him, *for His pleasure,* was an irritating consummation of man's love for God. Creating a chasm prevented this from ever happening. Jesus, paid the penalty for man's sin, the result of Satan's corruption, made atonement for man's sin, satisfying God's justice and opened the way for mankind to be reconciled to God. This trumped Satan's corruption of mankind and Jesus' atonement cast this reconciliation in stone. This is salvation. It is a stone bridge to God, all you have to do is cross it.

Were the angels aware of the seriousness of their decision to back Satan? Was Satan even aware of the consequences? Satan likely downplayed any consequences to the other angels, but surely he could not have foreseen such a bitter ending. Satan must have thought he had a good chance of succeeding, but could he have won even with 99% of the angels siding with him; he still would have had to overcome God himself? This could never have happened of course; if God would have lost 99% of His created angels, He would have foreseen it, and would have had a different plan.

Satan must have considered the consequences. Even eventually being in charge of such a vile and motley crew, in what seems to be the very opposite of a loving, caring, and worship filled place, a place of despair and *gnashing of teeth*, cannot come close to being a servant in God's domain. Even now do the angels fully understand what the lake of fire is? Whereas before, some at least were aiding and abetting Satan in his attacks on man, e.g. Job, Legion, and many other poor souls on earth, they were now all dedicated to disrupting God's plan of salvation. Even though Jesus had opened the door, mankind still had to *bend the knee* to Jesus and walk through the door. The fallen angels are working against mankind finding salvation. Does Satan crack the whip to ensure obedience, or did God transform them, leaving only negative desires and emotions, so they eagerly carry out their mission as Howard Pitman points out?

Now the duped angels may have fallen for Satan's wonderful promises, but certainly did not sign up to be *cast to earth* and then be cast into the lake of eternal fire. What would they do, grovel and plead with God? I would, anything but the lake of fire. It must already be a relatively miserable experience being cast out of God's heaven, where they *bathed* in His light and love. But there must have been more in the phrase *cast down to earth* than meets the eye.

We can understand that Satan was already totally irritated with God's focus on us humans and being assigned to minster to us; but nothing is said of the other angels aspiring to higher position, or being able to exercise more free will. Siding with Satan would presumably mean *less servitude* to God, and with that the opportunity for more pleasure through greater freedom.

With reason Satan, the devil, is in a rage, and the first letter of Peter leaves us in doubt about that.

1 Peter Chapter 5

[8]Be self-controlled and alert. Your enemy the devil prowls around like a roaring lion looking for someone to devour. [9]Resist him, standing firm in the faith, because you know that your brothers throughout the world are undergoing the same kind of sufferings.

But would the fallen angels, now called demons, have an inbuilt hatred for us. It certainly is not what I would have done, given the circumstances that we are told. The lake of fire was a one way trip, and God may have made it even worse if they continued to rebel against Him and His children. I think something happened in the process of being cast out of heaven. We have all seen the news reports of killers, who have been responsible for horrendous acts of murder and more; in the courtroom they show no remorse at all. Something is missing in them. It seems what love and compassion that they may have once had within them has gone, and they are left with whatever lust they are given over to. Could this be the same for the fallen angels, did God remove love, and all things of love from them? Nothing good is ever described about being thrown outside of God's heaven *where there is weeping and gnashing of teeth.* It does not sound like there is much, if any, love outside.

It seems also that in being cast down to earth, at the same instant when Jesus paid the price for our sins, the rebelling angels were transformed from angels of God's light to demons of darkness. How many angels were cast down to earth as demons?

Revelation Chapter 12

[3]Then another sign appeared in heaven: an enormous red dragon with seven heads and ten horns and seven crowns on his heads. [4]His tail swept a third of the stars out of the sky and flung them to the earth...

We see (in colourful terms), because of Satan, a third of the angels in heaven were *flung to earth*. Now, although this book does not describe all the debating points of why, it is widely accepted that the stars represent angels, and a third of the angels were cast out of heaven when they lost the war. Likening angels to stars is only a metaphor and in reality angels are angels and stars are stars, despite what some movies may have you believe. While we are on the subject we do not become angels when we die, we go to be with God in heaven.

Some angels were cast into a bottomless pit, for towards the end of the tribulation they are described as being set free to play their part, and this is described in great detail in the book of Revelation, the last book in the Bible. Were these the ones who assisted Satan in his torture of mankind in the Old Testament, just for sport? Maybe these ones have a vicious streak and are too violent for all but their role at the end of the tribulation. The Bible does not say who the angels who were chained in the bottomless pit were, or why they were chained there. So this is speculation.

Matthew Chapter 25

[31] "When the Son of Man comes in his glory, and all the angels with him, he will sit on his glorious throne. [32] All the nations will be gathered before him, and he will separate the people one from another as a shepherd separates the sheep from the goats. [33] He will put the sheep on his right and the goats on his left.

[34] *"Then the King will say to those on his right, 'Come, you who are blessed by my Father; take your inheritance, the kingdom prepared for you since the creation of the world.* [35] *For I was hungry and you gave me something to eat, I was thirsty and you gave me something to drink, I was a stranger and you invited me in,* [36] *I needed clothes and you clothed me, I was sick and you looked after me, I was in prison and you came to visit me.'*

[37] *"Then the righteous will answer him, 'Lord, when did we see you hungry and feed you, or thirsty and give you something to drink?* [38] *When did we see you a stranger and invite you in, or needing clothes and clothe you?* [39] *When did we see you sick or in prison and go to visit you?'*

[40] *"The King will reply, 'Truly I tell you, whatever you did for one of the least of these brothers and sisters of mine, you did for me.'*

[41] *"Then he will say to those on his left, 'Depart from me, you who are cursed, into the eternal fire prepared for the devil and his angels.* [42] *For I was hungry and you gave me nothing to eat, I was thirsty and you gave me nothing to drink,* [43] *I was a stranger and you did not invite me in, I needed clothes and you did not clothe me, I was sick and in prison and you did not look after me.'*

[44] *"They also will answer, 'Lord, when did we see you hungry or thirsty or a stranger or needing clothes or sick or in prison, and did not help you?'*

⁴⁵"He will reply, 'Truly I tell you, whatever you did not do for one of the least of these, you did not do for me.'

⁴⁶"Then they will go away to eternal punishment, but the righteous to eternal life."

Verse 41 assigns Satan and his angels to the *eternal fire*, which is the *lake of fire*, the destination for the *beast,* the *false prophet*, and eventually Satan. Note that the fallen angels, *his angels*, are already condemned. There is mention of mankind judging angels in Corinthians.

1 Corinthians Chapter 6

³Do you not know that we will judge angels? How much more the things of this life!

This verse tells us that God's judgment is just, as there is mention of statements to this effect in the courts of heaven in Revelation.

God's plan now turned to man. The fate of Satan and the fallen angels is sealed. Their free will no longer mattered. Their actions had already condemned them. Did God change them, or was it a natural consequence of being separated from the triune God; the Father is perfect, Jesus holds all creation together, and the Spirit is His Spirit. Whatever the mechanism, they seemed to have lost the essential element of love and compassion. Will those humans who fail to come into relationship with God suffer the same transformation;

will they be loveless destitute creatures, sharing their future Godless eternal home with Satan and all the fallen angels?

The Angels now took on a demonic purpose, attitude, and likely appearance. It seems that the fallen angels had lost any rights in the eyes of God as their actions had condemned them; God could use them in any way He wished. He didn't have to control them like puppets but merely 'adjust' the purpose in their heart. He knew how they would behave. Pleading would have done them no good, as it will be for anyone who does not opt for salvation. There is a time to choose and a time for consequences.

If this is so, it all fits in with what I think God's big picture plan is all about. The interaction between God and Satan in the first parts of the story of Job also seem to support this idea, and the scope and duration over which God's plan spans. The story of Job is the most puzzling WHY passage that I have pondered for decades. It makes sense that there are two phases of angels' interaction with man. First they were free in all the heavens, some siding with Satan and starting to question God, and episodes like that in Job occurred. Whether other angels were active in the torment of Job is unknown, but they were certainly active in blighting man, as Jesus spent a lot of time casting them out of people. This was so God could separate the angels just as He is separating man. Then lastly after the rebelling angels were cast down to earth they were openly hostile to man. This is so that mankind, already in a state of separation from God, has to demonstrate by his actions spurred by his heart, that he is reconciled to God through the salvation offered through Jesus. This hostile relationship between mankind and fallen angels has existed since the crucifixion, although some were openly hostile prior to that. They would appear to have a determined plan focused on thwarting all of God's efforts to bring His truth to man, and get as many people to come into relationship with Him. They are clever and very effective. Satan must be behind their efforts as there seems to be great skill and planning, but as always God limits his and his demon's authority. Once sealed by God, a person is under God's protection, and salvation cannot be lost; or can it?

Angels are not all created equal. When the rebelling angels were cast down to earth, it seems reasonable that some were literally transformed, or were naturally converted, to the angels that Revelation describes as being released from the bottomless pit.

Revelation Chapter 9

[1] The fifth angel sounded his trumpet, and I saw a star that had fallen from the sky to the earth. The star was given the key to the shaft of the Abyss. [2] When he opened the Abyss, smoke rose from it like the smoke from a gigantic furnace. The sun and sky were darkened by the smoke from the Abyss. [3] And out of the smoke locusts came down on the earth and were given power like that of scorpions of the earth. [4] They were told not to harm the grass of the earth or any plant or tree, but only those people who did not have the seal of God on their foreheads. [5] They were not allowed to kill them but

only to torture them for five months. And the agony they suffered was like that of the sting of a scorpion when it strikes. ⁶During those days people will seek death but will not find it; they will long to die, but death will elude them.

⁷The locusts looked like horses prepared for battle. On their heads they wore something like crowns of gold, and their faces resembled human faces. ⁸Their hair was like women's hair, and their teeth were like lions' teeth. ⁹They had breastplates like breastplates of iron, and the sound of their wings was like the thundering of many horses and chariots rushing into battle. ¹⁰They had tails with stingers, like scorpions, and in their tails they had power to torment people for five months. ¹¹They had as king over them the angel of the Abyss, whose name in Hebrew is Abaddon and in Greek is Apollyon (that is, Destroyer).

One final discussion about fallen angels; there is great theological debate referring to other sinning angels, apart from the rebelling angels. There are those who think that there were sexual relations between angels and women on earth who gave rise to a nation of giants. This is in Genesis, and there is another vague reference to angels in chains of darkness in 2 Peter, and another in Jude.

Genesis Chapter 6

¹When human beings began to increase in number on the earth and daughters were born to them, ²the sons of God saw that the daughters of humans were beautiful, and they married any of them they chose. ³Then the LORD said, "My

Spirit will not contend with humans forever, for they are mortal; their days will be a hundred and twenty years."

⁴The Nephilim were on the earth in those days—and also afterward—when the sons of God went to the daughters of humans and had children by them. They were the heroes of old, men of renown.

⁵The LORD saw how great the wickedness of the human race had become on the earth, and that every inclination of the thoughts of the human heart was only evil all the time. ⁶The LORD regretted that he had made human beings on the earth, and his heart was deeply troubled. ⁷So the LORD said, "I will wipe from the face of the earth the human race I have created—and with them the animals, the birds and the creatures that move along the ground—for I regret that I have made them." ⁸But Noah found favor in the eyes of the LORD.

2 Peter Chapter 2

⁴ For if God did not spare angels when they sinned, but sent them to hell, putting them into gloomy dungeons to be held for judgment;

Jude Chapter 1

⁶And the angels who did not keep their positions of authority but abandoned their own home—these he has kept in darkness, bound with everlasting chains for judgment on the great Day.

The word *angels* in all cases here probably refers to mankind; the original language can mean both. The context of this is sexual deviancy. Possibly referring to the population of the earth destroyed at the time of the flood. Some link this to the passage about *sons of God* and *daughters of men* in Genesis Chapter 6, and try to postulate that angels procreated with earthly women. There are a number of other ideas about what these passages mean, especially the passages in Genesis, but they are definitely not about angels procreating with earthly women.

Dog Days

When God told me I was like Jasmine, I took that to mean that I was disobedient. I accept that, but I hope it doesn't mean that I do not respond to correction. Jasmine, which is her polite name used for introductions, generally gets corrupted to Jazzbag, which more commonly suits her behaviour, or Jellybelly, when she is reclining, offering her big pink threadbare belly for a rub. She is definitely a Jazzbag when she thinks a belly rub should have been longer, and mischievously trots off with an air of retribution and returns with a slipper. This is not the 'dog fetching the slippers for her master' routine. She parades around the room, trophy in mouth, waiting for attention. If we ignore her she makes a big scene of only half pretending to chew it. If we try to coax her to bring it to one of us she stands, out of reach slipper in mouth, wagging her tail, while Clint Eastwood whistles 'the Good, the Bad, and the Ugly'. Stern voices make her drop it. I get up, pick up the slipper and wop her on the head, while pronouncing the sentence of 'BAD' upon her; she wags her tail and trots off to get another slipper.

Surely this is not a parallel of me and God! Do I shrug off discipline, maybe? Am I insensitive to God's guidance; has the top of my head become numb? It may not be slippers, but I'm sure I have a whole kit bag of habits that probably disappoint God more than irritate Him. Not evil things mind you, just stupid ways of expressing my independence that I do because I can, and because I can't feel the slipper that is slapping me on the head.

*Therefore rejoice, you heavens and you who dwell in them!
But woe to the earth and the sea, because the devil has
gone down to you! He is filled with fury because
he knows that his time is short."*

~ Revelation 12:12

THERE WAS WAR ON EARTH

The timing of the war in heaven had nothing to do with what I call war on earth. War on earth had two distinct phases, before and after the crucifixion of Jesus. The second phase is probably more intense than the first. Remember the age of mankind was just dawning. Our earth, our cradle, was ready, either after six literal days of God's work, or six periods spanning billions of years. Mankind was given life by God, and the knowledge of good and evil, by Satan. Pesky angels were locked up in the abyss at some point, but Satan and his rebelling angels were 'testing' mankind, and Satan was saying that we only worshiped God because He blessed us. Initially, up until the time of Jesus, and specifically His crucifixion, God tolerated Satan accusing mankind to His face, but He was playing Satan, using him to separate the angels. At the crucifixion the game was up, God cast them out of heaven. We are like the angels, we have free choice, but we are in an even worse position. We were separated from God at birth by our nature, being separated from God by the chasm of our inherently evil prone nature, and our ignorance of God; we could not see Him as the angels could. Although we can't see God, He says we can see Him in what He has created, presumably if our hearts are open. We have enough problems with our own nature, and are quite capable of making this earth a living hell all on our own, without Satan pacing the earth to *devour* us. What had we done to deserve Satan? Had God *sent* him to mess with us at the dawn of our birth?

Was there method in what I saw as madness? Why didn't God lock them all up, or throw them all in the lake of fire right then? Why *set* them on us? The angels, who could see God, had no doubt that He existed, and that He had almighty powers; He had created them, but some chose Satan. Through Satan, God had refined his angels; sorted the wheat from the chaff, sorted the angel sheep from the angel goats. If the angels, for whom God was so in their face, had to be sorted, we, who have to look carefully to see God, are a much more flakey proposition. God is Holy and cannot exist with evil in His presence. But how does God sort mankind out? Make us swear on the Bible to make promises we can't keep; or we could lie through our teeth. "I swear allegiance to Almighty God, who made me (unless I feel like doing something just a little bad)." I wouldn't trust that; would God? What was God to do?

Would He stand on the street corner, and declare, "The end of the world is nigh, judgement time is coming soon, and I will sort the people who love Me and My ways, from all the rest who do not live the best way to live, the way I have shown them, and who do not care a fig about My Majesty"? Would He send His son Jesus, who gave up His power and was born as a human, so He could demonstrate that He could live a Holy and loving life in the midst of corruption and evil? Would He make Jesus wait till He was thirty, the age that the Jewish culture considered the minimum for maturity, so people would even listen to Him? Would He give Him miracles to do in the power of the Father, to help people understand that only God could do these things so He must be God? *Yes*, He would. But this was after generations of prophets and Kings whom He had anointed to speak His words to the people, urging them to repent, to turn away from their evil ways of greed, jealousy, lies, stealing, and even murder, and embrace a holy life, or at least to try to live it.

The problem with the evil is that it is from us, inside us, but it is encouraged by Satan and his demons. We are very susceptible to Satan, and to say that he leads us into evil with extreme prejudice is not an exaggeration. It is not from God, and God gives us the tools to overcome the temptation in this world, but it is we who, with or without Satan, commit the evil. God restricts what Satan and his demons are allowed to do in this world; He doesn't restrict us.

Luke Chapter 20

[9] He went on to tell the people this parable: "A man planted a vineyard, rented it to some farmers and went away for a long time. [10] At harvest time he sent a servant to the tenants so they would give him some of the fruit of the vineyard. But the tenants beat him and sent him away empty-handed. [11] He sent another servant, but that one also they beat and treated shamefully and sent away empty-handed. [12] He sent still a third, and they wounded him and threw him out.

¹³ "Then the owner of the vineyard said, 'What shall I do? I will send my son, whom I love; perhaps they will respect him.'

¹⁴ "But when the tenants saw him, they talked the matter over. 'This is the heir,' they said. 'Let's kill him, and the inheritance will be ours.' ¹⁵So they threw him out of the vineyard and killed him.

"What then will the owner of the vineyard do to them? ¹⁶He will come and kill those tenants and give the vineyard to others."

When the people heard this, they said, "God forbid!"

¹⁷Jesus looked directly at them and asked, "Then what is the meaning of that which is written:

"'The stone the builders rejected has become the cornerstone'?

¹⁸Everyone who falls on that stone will be broken to pieces; anyone on whom it falls will be crushed."

In this parable, it is likely that the tenants are the religious leaders in the Jewish culture; the vines are God's chosen nation, the Jews. The servants and the son, whom the vineyard owner sent, are the prophets, and His son is Jesus. This is a parable spoken by Jesus, and is a précis of the history of the Jews, their future, including the crucifixion of Jesus.

The law handed down to Moses was straightforward and reasonable, but could not be kept by man, demonstrating to the Jews that they could not be holy in their own strength. God knew this, and it was part of His plan, and He sent prophets to try to steer the people in the right direction and to highlight their failure. Meanwhile under the Judges, Kings, and the emerging religious elite the Pharisees and Sadducees, the majority of the Jewish nation not only turned a deaf ear to God, but actively sought to worship other gods. God punished the nation a number of times, even bringing war to their doorstep from powerful emerging empires All the time He was sorting them through exile with only the faithful returning, and eventually complete dispersion under the Romans after the Church was birthed.

These rebellious people were ruled by a legalistic Pharisee elite, who were in turn ruled by the occupying Romans. The Romans provided an enforced *peace* over a large portion of the civilized world all around the Mediterranean, and this was the setting into which Jesus was born. The Pharisees had expanded the Ten Commandments, and other cultural processes into over six hundred rules. The net effect was a legalistic society, ruled by a hypocritical elite. Almost nothing of *'Love the Lord your God, with all your heart and with all your soul and with all your strength and with all your mind'; and, 'Love your neighbor as yourself* 'from Luke Chapter 10 verse 27 was left.

Jesus was a radical in the eyes of the Pharisees, with teachings that reached back to the roots of the Jewish faith, and put love of God and each other back in the forefront, not so much deposing the six hundred manmade rules as making them irrelevant. In His own words He said;

Matthew Chapter 9

[16]"No one sews a patch of unshrunk cloth on an old garment, for the patch will pull away from the garment, making the tear worse. [17]Neither do men pour new wine into old wineskins. If they do, the skins will burst, the wine will run out and the wineskins will be ruined. No, they pour new wine into new wineskins, and both are preserved."

This meant His new teaching could not be accommodated by the old religion, and they had to come to it afresh. He was hinting at His new church, which would not be under the old regime, but be built upon Him for its new foundations, a New Covenant. The major difference now was that people could come to God by the salvation provided by Jesus, through faith, and not by works, which was a hopeless task under the Pharisees. The reasonable, but burdensome Mosaic Law, was not done away with, but Jesus offered a way to be righteous in the sight of God when they failed to live up to it.

Even after Jesus had healed thousands during His time of ministry, and revealed the Love of God in refreshing new ways, the Jews were led astray through the deceit of Satan. The religious leaders clearly saw their way of life being threatened by Jesus' teachings and sought to rid themselves of Jesus. The leaders found Jesus guilty at a kangaroo court but they could not hand down a death sentence, only the

Roman *justice* could do that. The leaders, and Satan, urged the crowd to demand the death sentence from Pilot, a ruthless Roman prefect. Even Pilot, who was no particular friend of Jesus, but had been warned by his wife because of a dream, washed his hands of the crucifixion, but authorized it anyway.

If Satan was working against God the Father and Jesus, why did God allow it? It was all part of the plan! From the beginning, even in the third Chapter of the first book in the Bible,

Genesis Chapter 3

^{15}And I will put enmity between you and the woman, and between your offspring and hers; he will crush your head, and you will strike his heel."

Speaking of the serpent Satan, God says that he, Satan, will strike the heel of the offspring of a woman, that is Jesus, but Jesus will crush Satan's head. Jesus is Spirit, and spirit cannot die, like our flesh dies. Spurring on Jesus' crucifixion, *killing his body*, only strikes His heel. Did Satan not understand that Hell could not hold the innocent and Holy Jesus? Satan wouldn't have even been aware that Jesus would die with the burden of the world's sin upon Him, or did he just want Jesus to return to heaven. But Satan has been set up for an ambush, as He is dying, God lays the world's sin on Jesus and He pays God's penalty, which we cannot fully comprehend, but it opened the door to God's grace through salvation. The Age of Grace had begun. But still in the future is Satan's fate, and being thrown into the lake of fire Jesus crushes Satan's head.

In this episode of God's plan, during the war on earth, God had allowed Satan to guide the Romans to establish their empire, which included all of Israel, which they called Palestine, and establish Pax Romana, a relatively peaceful time, due to widespread Roman occupation, between 27BC and 180AD. Satan thought he was dealing a great blow to God's plan but had merely, even though at great cost to the Father and Jesus, ushered in the age of Jesus' Church. Satan had been played again. I bet he was steaming mad and some demons got a tail-lashing that day. During the Pax Romana, the Romans had built roads all over the known world, even as far as England. The modern day London was the lowest point where you could ford the river Thames, and there, around 50AD, they established a fortification they called Londinium.

When the great persecution began in Jerusalem, these roads and the brutal peace enabled the apostles and the thousands of mostly Jews, who had become Christians, to take the Gospel, the good news of salvation by grace, to the rest of the world. I wonder if it was Satan's plan to stamp out the Church before it got going by fostering the persecution of the Church in Jerusalem, the people of the Way as they were called then. No doubt there is a dot there. God seemed to reverse every plan of Satan, maybe that is part of His punishment; it must just reinforce his growing awareness of just how inferior he is compared with God.

The Church spread like wild fire, to the entire known world and even became the Roman state religion in 380AD under the edict of Thessalonica by the emperor Theodosius. What great timing, what a great plan to have Jesus start His Church in this period; a coincidence, I think not. It seems whatever Satan did, just made the Church grow.

Did you know that the greatest expansion of the Christian Church happens in times of persecution? The Church is exploding in all the access restricted nations in Asia. China has between 100 and 200 million Christians, despite putting congregations and their pastors in prison and demolishing their churches. In India there are some temples that although they look like Sikh temples are actually churches where the people have found Jesus and are worshiping Him in what were Sikh temples; it is the same in some mosques. Jesus is revealing Himself through dreams and visions and winning people groups to Himself. All over Indo-China the Church is growing rapidly with the minimum of resources. In the West, after the rapid declines at the start of the age of materialism, the Church is on the rise again; people having discovered that materialism provides a very thin veneer of happiness.

The multi-dimensional stage is where the war that was fought in heaven, and now moved to earth, lingers on. It is now fully open season on humans on earth; not just Satan, but billions of demons roam around to try and devour us. So having a better understanding of the lead up to the war on earth, and showing that we are the prize being fought over by

Satan and his demons, and God, and His angels, I think can explain why God effectively set Satan and his demons on us.

The clues come from the story of Job, and the big *why* of God playing Satan to test Job, when God knew Job was a true servant of His, and would not buckle under Satan's torment. God knows everything, Satan does not. When you have a hand of cards that holds all the masters, or aces, depending on the game, you rule the game; you can see the future and control it. You can *play* your opponent. I don't know why God played Satan in the Job story, but play him, He did. Notice that after his first return, Satan does not come back to argue about Job anymore. Maybe Satan was punished by the defeat, like he is every time his plans backfire. He was so certain he could turn Job against God, probably snickering about how easy it would be; after all, didn't he think he was almost equal with God Himself? Maybe this small defeat brought God glory, and Satan punishing humiliation, possibly the worst pain he could suffer apart from the lake of fire. When pride gets deflated it's painful. The take away here is that God played Satan.

Far from being a saboteur, Satan is a major part of God's plan. He is limited in his powers and resources, and has his strings pulled, and his buttons pushed by God like a goat herder steers his herd with a stick. Satan or one of his demons will probably read this book, he may or may not agree, but either way God wins. If he agrees, he loses in the same way as he lost with Job, if he doesn't, he is all the more deluded and easier to control.

I think Satan is definitely being punished as he fails in this war against God. Every defeat shows him how inadequate he is, and now being denied audiences with God, being exiled, I'm sure he feels the pain of his great fall every day. His pride is severely damaged and his arrogance only a shadow of when he was enticing the angels to rebel against God. Now, knowing his sentence, he has a single purpose to his existence; to take out his rage on us, and try to frustrate God's plans, if that were even possible.

Do you start to see the big picture? Yet there is another element to all this, not only is Satan being played so God's plan unfolds on time, and in the way He wants, but Satan has another pivotal role during this whole age of grace.

Dog Days

Half the days are often deeply overcast in the winter. Today was just another of those days. My wife and I share a car and I was driving her across our massive concrete floating bridge into town. Jasmine was reclining on a rear seat as I made a leisurely left turn across three oncoming lanes. I was in no hurry, the traffic was all going in my direction, and the only oncoming car was a long way off. As I entered the oncoming inside lane an SUV appeared out of nowhere, just 15 feet away; we met corner to corner. No one was seriously hurt, just some bumps and bruises. Disaster or Blessing?

Our car was about to need thousands of dollars in general maintenance; a few thousand we didn't have. Since I gave my life to Jesus, and gave up my desire for riches, we have lived a life of extremes as far as money goes. Currently we are in a financial dip. This has never bothered us as God takes care of us, as He says He would in Malachi if we tithe. My old Subaru was only worth about three to five thousand if I sold it, but we had new ice tires and years previously I had spent thousands 'fixing it up'.

It was a right-off, the insurance payout was nine thousand three hundred; the doors of God's storehouse in heaven sure opened wide that day, just as He promised. We now have a fully serviced Ford Escape 4x4 with half the mileage on it as our Subaru. It is in much better shape than the Subaru with almost new sets of summer and winter tires; we also pocketed thousands. Now that's God's economy.

"Do not suppose that I have come to bring peace to the earth. I did not come to bring peace, but a sword."

~ Matthew 10:34

THE BATTLEFIELD

It is hard to get people to commit to anything. With only one opinion, declaration, or manifesto it is hard to quantify the level of agreement there is to it. Political parties nearly always come in two major flavours. Where there are a number of parties, the platforms get blurred and overlap; there is no clear choice and unstable coalitions form. For God to just stand by Himself, declare His ways, His truths, and ask mankind to make a choice, it would be far from black and white. God did not make this earth to be a happiness opportunity, to strive for the dream of owning a home, raising a family, owning two or more cars, taking two vacations a year, and stashing money away to carry on a pleasurable lifestyle until you die. Our lives are *the* opportunity that God provides for us to choose Him, or not.

God provided two poles in heaven for the angels, Himself and Satan. The battlefield was on a slope, God was at the bottom with the angels. This is because the angels could see God and had no doubt that He created them, and so were naturally biased towards Him. They had to explicitly choose Satan who tried to convince them, against their natural bias towards God, to rebel. On earth, despite the abundance of subtle fingerprints of God in our world, we do not see God, with all the distractions in our lives it is not obvious without making an effort to find Him, that He was our creator; hence all the debates. Satan is present as the other polarizing agent, but in this case the playing field is sloped the other way; we are at the bottom and God is at the top. By default we are against God, this is our nature; we want to be in charge, beholden to no one. By nature we are selfish, don't like rules, and want to exercise our self-proclaimed *right* of self-determination. We find God's rules at least somewhat restrictive, if not fundamentally opposed to us having the most self-serving fun we can get out of this life.

We have to make a concerted effort to move toward God, against the natural bias Satan has set up in this world which works very effectively with our corrupted *fallen* nature; Satan created the tinsel of this world to perfectly resonate with our nature. Satan has set obstacles on the slope up towards God. Satan is there, with his demons, to *snatch away* the word of God from those focussed on themselves, to let it drift out of other's lives when the next interesting thing comes along, to wear us down with the burdens of this life; raising a family, finding and keeping a job, paying the bills etc. But for those who feel that something is missing in their lives, those who are searching, they find a way to move up the slope, overcome the pitfalls and traps set by Satan, and engage God. Their lives are still lived on the slope, but with the Holy Spirit partnering with their spirit, they are given wisdom and strength to stand against temptation, and survive their falls with the grace of God. With perseverance, and trust in a God who has their back, those people gradually start to see Satan working in this world and are able to avoid him. One of

Satan's greatest powers is that he wants to be invisible and loves it when people do not even believe he exists.

God does not want drifters, people who are attracted to His message one moment, then drift to the next piece of tinsel that takes their fancy. God does not want people to accept Him, but then take no stand, and not become active; to be a *lukewarmer*. He does not want debaters, even this book should not detract believers from *seeking His kingdom*; God wants soldiers! You cannot be a spectator, this is WAR, if you are on God's side you are a soldier automatically, you are expected to fight, and you should know that someone is out to get you. You get to pick your side, actively to side with God, or side with Satan by default, and live with the consequences.

Matthew Chapter 10

34 "Do not suppose that I have come to bring peace to the earth. I did not come to bring peace, but a sword. 35 For I have come to turn 'a man against his father, a daughter against her mother, a daughter-in-law against her mother-in-law — 36 a man's enemies will be the members of his own household.'"

God does not want you to make a flippant choice; He wants you to make a dead serious choice. He wants you to argue about it, fight about it with your family. He wants you to *think* about it, beyond the distractions of this world, which cry out "don't waste your time on God stuff; we are the most important thing to spend your time on." Actions speaking louder than words, is never more true than taking sides.

Making a verbal commitment but not following through with a life that lives that commitment is just not good enough. Some people call them, *closet Christians*, or even *pew polishers*; Jesus calls them lukewarm.

Revelation Chapter 3

[15] I know your deeds, that you are neither cold nor hot. I wish you were either one or the other! [16] So, because you are lukewarm--neither hot nor cold--I am about to spit you out of my mouth.

When the judgment comes, for those whose names are not written in the Lamb's book of life, God wants solid evidence, not flimsy evidence. His Justice must and will be self-evident. He polarizes the battlefield, this world in which we make our choices, so that we are clearly on the side of God, or by inaction, part of the world Satan has created through the millennia by the manipulation of man, while all the time being played by God to polarize the world to perfection.

In this next passage, the great prostitute, Babylon, is referenced as all that is evil and corrupt in this world. Satan, his demons, and all those not written in the Lamb's book of life have been judged for rebellion against God and their sinful deeds.

Revelation Chapter 19

[1] After this I heard what sounded like the roar of a great multitude in heaven shouting: "Hallelujah! Salvation and

glory and power belong to our God, ^{2}for true and just are his judgments. He has condemned the great prostitute who corrupted the earth by her adulteries. He has avenged on her the blood of his servants." ^{3}And again they shouted: "Hallelujah! The smoke from her goes up forever and ever."

How else could you get one percent in almost every culture, envied by the rest, and often vilified by the remaining ninety nine percent, while striving to have what they have. There may be various lusts like control, power, etc., but they always seem to be accompanied by money. In many respects money is power, money can buy a person's vision of the way they want things to be. Money often buys independence from God, even for a dedicated Christian, maybe unintentionally. It is next to impossible to be dependent on God when you are wealthy, when wealth inherently provides choices that are lacking if you are poor.

Mark Chapter 10

^{17}As Jesus started on his way, a man ran up to him and fell on his knees before him. "Good teacher," he asked, "what must I do to inherit eternal life?"

^{18}"Why do you call me good?" Jesus answered. "No one is good—except God alone.

^{19}You know the commandments: 'You shall not murder, you shall not commit adultery, you shall not steal, you shall not give false testimony, you shall not defraud, honor your father and mother'."

[20] *"Teacher," he declared, "all these I have kept since I was a boy."*

[21] *Jesus looked at him and loved him. "One thing you lack," he said. "Go, sell everything you have and give to the poor, and you will have treasure in heaven. Then come, follow me."*

[22] *At this the man's face fell. He went away sad, because he had great wealth.*

[23] *Jesus looked around and said to his disciples, "How hard it is for the rich to enter the kingdom of God!"* [24] *The disciples were amazed at his words. But Jesus said again, "Children, how hard it is to enter the kingdom of God.* [25] *It is easier for a camel to go through the eye of a needle than for someone who is rich to enter the kingdom of God."*

[26] *The disciples were even more amazed, and said to each other, "Who then can be saved?"*

[27] *Jesus looked at them and said, "With man this is impossible, but not with God; all things are possible with God."*

[28] *Then Peter spoke up, "We have left everything to follow you!"*

[29] *"Truly I tell you," Jesus replied, "no one who has left home or brothers or sisters or mother or father or children or fields for me and the gospel*

³⁰will fail to receive a hundred times as much in this present age: homes, brothers, sisters, mothers, children and fields—along with persecutions—and in the age to come eternal life.

³¹But many who are first will be last, and the last first."

The battlefield is not nice, it is not even flat. It has traps, mines and potholes. It's like having two poles of a magnet and a ball bearing; you are the ball bearing, and although you are bouncing around in the battlefield, you are going to be attracted and migrate to one pole or the other, even though one way is easier than the other. It's almost impossible to balance yourself in the middle, although many churchgoers try to do just that. Many people are *Sunday* Christians, they go to church on Sunday, but when they go to work on Monday none of their colleagues would ever have known.

Matthew Chapter 13

³Then he told them many things in parables, saying: "A farmer went out to sow his seed. ⁴As he was scattering the seed, some fell along the path, and the birds came and ate it up. ⁵Some fell on rocky places, where it did not have much soil. It sprang up quickly, because the soil was shallow. ⁶But when the sun came up, the plants were scorched, and they withered because they had no root. ⁷Other seed fell among thorns, which grew up and choked the plants. ⁸Still other seed fell on good soil, where it produced a crop—a hundred, sixty or thirty times what was sown. ⁹Whoever has ears, let them hear."

For God, commitment is everything. If you commit, you are able to stay the course, which is the proving ground for your commitment. If you have commitment you will live in the ways God says, it will not be easy, but you will have an invisible force with you; where do you think the concepts of the *Force* in Star Wars came from? Satan is not randomly going about the earth looking for people to distract, snare, or lure away from being a participant in this war; he wants you to be inactive, he has a plan, and in that plan are many strategies. Nothing is the way it seems, a good life can give you all the things that the world, Satan's domain, tells you that you deserve and need. Your life is a mixture of ups and downs, but at least you have all the right stuff for a good life, right? Do you have enough money, for now and in the future, good; do you worry about it, is the stock market your friend? Does your money manager take the burden off your shoulders; do you get a shock when you read your portfolio statement? Everyone knows that life is never a bed of roses, and there are countless things that continually go wrong and demand your attention to fix, or worry about if you can't fix them. These are the thorns and thistles in the Bible passage above. The thorns and thistles are planted, they are land mines, and they are just one way that Satan stops you focusing on having a committed life, or to stop you even thinking about a commitment.

Like two generals, each on their own hilltop overlooking the battlefield, they give their orders, as they roll out their battle plans, and constantly react to the other general's tactics. On one side is Satan, he directs his efforts on the people who are opposing him and making a difference. The others, those people busy tending to their lives, oblivious to the war, he ignores, they are his by default and of course they can easily be collateral damage as he ravages this world. Satan not only wages war in real time, but has also prepared the physical battlefield itself, these are the cultures of this world, that imprison people, like the Indian caste system, and the tinsel of western culture, which is now infecting Asia. Satan thinks he has really got the upper hand, not only is our world infested with every type of filth, like pornography, to stimulate our base nature, but he also has legion upon legion of demons to fuel excursions to the *dark side*. Satan has landscaped the battlefield under God's careful eye, ensuring Satan meets God's exacting requirements. God is on the other side, His angels defend people from unfair attacks by Satan's demons, but neither can go against the free will of the billions of people milling around on the battlefield. Both angels and demons do the will of their masters, but demons lie and cheat, and use deceit with great skill. There is a demon specialized in every failing a human can have; they are experts, not generalists.

Think how successful a con-artist would be if he started cleverer than anyone else on earth, but was able to experiment with us for thousands of years. None of us would be able to withstand his tricks. But with the Holy Spirit in us, Jesus says we can. Once a person makes a commitment to Jesus, believes in the sacrifice He made for them, the Holy

Spirit comes into their life, He lives within them. As long as that person does not turn their back on Jesus, the Holy Spirit will stay with them, to guide them, and be their conduit between them and God. The Holy Spirit is their phone line to God, but the voice which God uses is rarely audible, He speaks the language of life. He has made those who believe in Him overcomers; able to overcome Satan's temptations. He helps them and limits Satan.

Without Satan on the battlefield there is no battle. It is a muddle of billions wandering around. It is Satan who dresses up this world through billions of his willing human workers. Satan has made up the rules of this world, carefully crafted them and the cultures that are manifestations of our human nature, often our base nature. Look out for number one, get your share, lie a little, lie a lot, admit who you are and simply cheat, stab someone in the back if you have to, if you don't they will. The world we live in is not neutral; it is made up of people who do these things, with Satan helping them succeed by using his influence where it suits his plan. Often after helping you along in your devious schemes, just when it's all coming together, he pulls the rug out from under you. Your cries of sadness and anguish are music to his ears and it's the thought of hearing it that gets him up on a Monday morning; distraction, distraction, lust, lust.

No one is free. Satan has enough demons to mess with everyone who lets one or more into their lives. We just seem to be made to have something in us, the Holy Spirit, or an unholy spirit, a demon. Any type of thought that is not pure, if we dwell on it, can open the door to a demon to assist us in developing that thought. Our mind wanders to lustful things, not necessarily sexual, we envy someone else's stuff, or our eyes dwell on something impure and out goes the welcome mat for a specialist to guide our thoughts. Demons don't just hang around us waving their hands and chanting things to influence us, they can inhabit us. They talk to each other, not about the weather, they strategize. We even see that intelligence about Jesus and even Paul had spread throughout the demon ranks.

Acts Chapter 19

[13]Some Jews who went around driving out evil spirits tried to invoke the name of the Lord Jesus over those who were demon-possessed. They would say, "In the name of Jesus, whom Paul preaches, I command you to come out." [14]Seven sons of Sceva, a Jewish chief priest, were doing this. [15][One day] the evil spirit answered them, Jesus I know, and I know about Paul, but who are you?" [16]Then the man who had the evil spirit jumped on them and overpowered them all. He gave them such a beating that they ran out of the house naked and bleeding.

Demons are spirits, angels are spirit, even God is Spirit; they live in the second or third heavens. Although there are hints of time, space, and distance there, matter as we know it, required for a fleshly body, doesn't appear to exist. Although we can't see them, it seems our mortal bodies of flesh have the capacity to host spirits; we have a spirit, we can accommodate the Holy Spirit, why not others. In more than one place the Bible indicates a person can host more than one spirit, somehow join with them in the part of the second heaven that envelops the first heaven, earth. Joined in time and space, it may allow the unseen world of spirits, our spirit, the Holy Spirit, God's angels, and the demons, to have intimate contact with us and influence us. You do realize that the little demon in red and the little angel in white sitting on our shoulders is a joke, right? But still we seem to have this innate understanding, that God and probably demons *talk* to us. How many demons can you fit on the head of your pin?

Mark Chapter 5

[1]They went across the lake to the region of the Gerasenes. [2]When Jesus got out of the boat, a man with an impure spirit came from the tombs to meet him. [3]This man lived in the tombs, and no one could bind him anymore, not even with a chain. [4]For he had often been chained hand and foot, but he tore the chains apart and broke the irons on his feet. No one was strong enough to subdue him. [5]Night and day among the tombs and in the hills he would cry out and cut himself with stones.

[6]When he saw Jesus from a distance, he ran and fell on his knees in front of him. [7]He shouted at the top of his voice, "What do you want with me, Jesus, Son of the Most High God? In God's name don't torture me!" [8]For Jesus had said to him, "Come out of this man, you impure spirit!"

[9]Then Jesus asked him, "What is your name?"

"My name is Legion," he replied, "for we are many." ^{10}*And he begged Jesus again and again not to send them out of the area.*

^{11}*A large herd of pigs was feeding on the nearby hillside.* ^{12}*The demons begged Jesus, "Send us among the pigs; allow us to go into them."* ^{13}*He gave them permission, and the impure spirits came out and went into the pigs. The herd, about two thousand in number, rushed down the steep bank into the lake and was drowned.*

A bad day for the pigs; it would seem that even animals can host spirits. Although not the subject of this book, the *do animals go to heaven* question is answered in part by the following passage, but be beware of subtle misinterpretation due to translation. Maybe it's a dot for another book; read carefully the second sentence in verse 5.

Genesis Chapter 9

^{4}*"But you must not eat meat that has its lifeblood still in it.* ^{5}*And for your lifeblood I will surely demand an accounting. I will demand an accounting from every animal. And from each man, too, I will demand an accounting for the life of his fellow man.*

Dog Days

Jasmine loves cuddles; or more correctly likes to be rubbed, caressed; almost any affection demonstrated to any part of her woolly body. I sit and gaze out across the lake, watching as the white claws of winter creep over the peaks of the mountains on the other side. I am pausing between paragraphs and Jasmine rouses from lying near my feet, stretches from four feet to six feet as she breathes out her sleep through a yawning mouth. She ambles around to the empty part of the sofa and bumbles aboard. Mostly she sits and faces me with that infinite stare (or vacant look), but sometimes she sits and leans back on the sofa mimicking me.

It's all a trap, she looks so cute so I put my arm around her shoulders and rub her chest. As I rub she starts to go into jelly mode. It's as if her bones and muscle become jelly and she collapses sideways onto my lap, writing a few words of gibberish on my keyboard. As I continue to rub her, the more she turns into jelly and we enter the rub-arama phase.

She seems to go into a coma as she gradually contours to my lap on her back. Her head gradually flows off my lap and runs down my leg, appropriately followed by the rest of her woolly bag of jelly onto the floor.

"Go! I am sending you out like lambs among wolves."

~ Luke 10:3

Psy-Ops

Psychological Operations, Psy-Ops, is a term I first heard in the Starship Troopers movie. In the movie earth was being bombarded from a distant planet by giant insects shooting equally giant plasma-balls from their bodies and destroying whole cities on earth. It was mankind against monster insects, but there was a hidden menace, there was an insect hiding inside the planet that had a huge brain; it was time for the Psy-Ops guys. Dressed in long leather trench coats and resembling the SS nasties from the Second World War, these Psy-Ops officers were after the brains behind the insect beasties.

Almost every country now has cyber and anti-cyber departments engaged in cyber warfare, trying to locate and neutralize enemy cyber forces, in the spider web-like maze that the combatants hide in. The internet is their highway and the battles are brain against brain. The weapons are sophisticated but malicious programs constructed to infiltrate the defenses of the enemy and like sleeper cells, lie in wait on unsuspecting people's computers to be activated, sometimes by the millions within seconds to prevent the enemy responding to the threat in time. At other times, the perpetrator attacks an individual computer system or network and little by little gains access to steal or wreak havoc.

Satan and his demons operate in similar ways, but are much more elusive; they also have much more power. Like cyber-hackers, Satan by far prefers to remain invisible, not only to our eyes, but also to our minds. He works at remaining a myth, a figment of a sci-fi movie maker's imagination. By often ridiculing himself, he maintains the illusion that you must be mad to believe in him. The Christian Fundamentalists have made themselves a target for the brainwashed masses he has deceived. Some Christian groups attract the label of fanatic in this regard and understandably there is little mention of Satan in mainline churches wishing to avoid the tar brush; even the Lord's Prayer has been de-demonized by the line "and keep us from the evil one," being commuted to "and keep us from evil."

The Bible is far from silent about Satan, but who reads the Bible anymore, or if they do, who doesn't selectively edit it? If you believe in angels then you had better believe in Satan; he *is* an angel. Now sentenced, as the leader of the angel rebellion in God's heaven, and subsequently cast down to earth with one third of the angels who followed him, he is barred from God's heaven and is now the prince of the 'air', roaming our earth. He is assumed to be the leader of the ongoing campaign against man, and as a group they are referred to as the fallen angels. Satan is also referred to as the beast, the dragon, serpent, and evil one. Jesus referred to him as the father of lies; lying being his native language.

Just because he lies constantly, does not make him stupid. One third of the angels believed his lies and went up against their Creator; perhaps numbering in the billions. This is not a farfetched number as Jesus referred to children having a guardian angel; there are over two billion children in the world today. Satan was a top if not the top angel. He has a superb intellect, he blows any human away. It would also seem that he and the other fallen angels were transformed in some way when they were cast down to earth; they seem to have lost any love or compassion they once may have had. At a stretch, they may have had God's Holy Spirit joined to their spirit, as Christians do on earth; if this was so, the Holy Spirit was stripped from them, removing God's light from their lives. Either way, they would appear to have it in for us. Working under strategic orders from Satan, or with a mission giving them freedom to work against anyone searching for Jesus or performing kingdom work, there could be more demons than humans.

Their 'air' is some sort of parallel realm from which our realm is not only visible but readily accessible; remember Jesus spoke to the many demons called Legion inhabiting a human in our realm. They are spirit, but can attach themselves to, or inhabit, human and animal beings; just as we have *our* spirit attached to *our* bodies and can also accommodate the Holy Spirit. Once inhabiting a being they seem to have much greater influence, although this may manifest itself as conflict; Jesus let the 'Legion' of demons go from the man into a herd of pigs, which immediately ran over a cliff into the sea.

Demons are constricted, limited by God in what they can do. Some are currently constrained in chains, in the abyss, the bottomless pit; maybe they are too destructive. God has posted angels on earth to protect us, and maybe to prevent demons from overstepping their allowed scope. They can hear, think, and seem ever diligent in their task to disrupt kingdom work. As in the case of Legion, a whole bunch of demons who called themselves Legion, inhabited a man living amongst the tombs near a pagan town besides the Sea of Galilee, where there seemed to be no active kingdom work taking place. Legion was just happy to violently take over the man's life and create fear among the local population. Jesus could read man's thoughts (maybe with God's help as He had set his powers aside); there is a very good chance that demons can also. They seem to be able to implant thought, even if they do not inhabit a person. Who knows how influential they are if they inhabit someone who may be completely taken over, demon *possessed*. Either from the outside or inside they can act as thought amplifiers, reinforcing our own thoughts, or forcefully instigating completely foreign thought processes; that's why it's dangerous to dwell on evil thoughts that enter our minds.

Paul warns us to be ever wary about what we let enter our minds. Our minds are already full of evil or distracting junk; every day the world tries to pump more into us. Jesus says once we receive the Holy Spirit, the process of renewing our minds starts. It's one of the ways that we get to overcome temptation and be sensitive to Satan's plans and tricks; we start to see the trees in the forest. If Paul warned us to be extra diligent about what we let enter our minds 2,000 years ago, when they didn't even have newspapers, and very few images of anything anywhere, what would he say to us with 24/7 bombardment of subversive images that we don't even go looking for. Men are particularly susceptible to any image with a sexual theme; why do you think manufacturers use scantily clad girls to help them get your attention when trying to sell you their cars?

Our brain works like an automatic Google. Think of a topic and our brain automatically retrieves related images or concepts and flashes them in front of our eyes. It's like our brain throws pictures at the windows of our consciousness to see what sticks. If we dwell on it, it enhances the picture like an MPEG picture becoming more in focus by the second, or automatically hitting the *more like this* button on our computer. In a fraction of a second we get sucked in and get engrossed in a tailor made fantasy consisting of real memories or images we have seen, or both. Satan knows and has told his demons how our brains work. He has filled this world through every imaginable medium with music, images, and words, and infused any non-mind-polluting content with his garbage as advertisements. Almost all TV and streaming video has ads, because the owners of the media want to make money. In ads almost anything goes, as long as the media ratings are maintained. Living in today's world we are closer to the Matrix movie construct than we think; most of the world is being played like puppets by Satan and his media crew. Invisibly surrounding us, they make adjustments to what images flash into our minds in real time, depending where our conscious thought patterns are taking us. The term *we are not alone* is an understatement. For all his pride, Satan's intellect overrules his pride when it comes to suggestion, he knows that we resist being told what to do, and he is most skilled at making us think that everything we think of is by our choice; who's the arrogant one?

Howard Pitman includes a short animation on his website, a recreation of what he claims to have seen, that shows a grotesque demon, somewhat like a 3 foot frog, entering a man who is engaged in conversation with a young lady. I think the inference is that dwelling on evil thoughts makes us vulnerable to demons entering us. There are many warnings about protecting our thoughts, and avoiding any contact with occult activities, such as the Ouija board, and people who engage in these things. The Bible explicitly states that 'sorcerers', who are people who try to communicate with spirits and the dead, will never enter God's heaven. Modern day sorcerers are people who attend or hold séances, write horoscopes, act as mediums, play with Ouija boards, etc.

It wasn't just Jesus who cast demons out of possessed people. When Jesus sent out the 70 disciples that He had empowered, they returned with their own stories.

Luke Chapter 10

[1]*After this the Lord appointed seventy-two others and sent them two by two ahead of him to every town and place where*

he was about to go. ²He told them, "The harvest is plentiful, but the workers are few. Ask the Lord of the harvest, therefore, to send out workers into his harvest field. ³Go! I am sending you out like lambs among wolves. ⁴Do not take a purse or bag or sandals; and do not greet anyone on the road.

⁵"When you enter a house, first say, 'Peace to this house.' ⁶If someone who promotes peace is there, your peace will rest on them; if not, it will return to you. ⁷Stay there, eating and drinking whatever they give you, for the worker deserves his wages. Do not move around from house to house.

⁸"When you enter a town and are welcomed, eat what is offered to you. ⁹Heal the sick who are there and tell them, 'The kingdom of God has come near to you.' ¹⁰But when you enter a town and are not welcomed, go into its streets and say, ¹¹'Even the dust of your town we wipe from our feet as a warning to you. Yet be sure of this: The kingdom of God has come near.' ¹²I tell you, it will be more bearable on that day for Sodom than for that town.

¹³"Woe to you, Chorazin! Woe to you, Bethsaida! For if the miracles that were performed in you had been performed in Tyre and Sidon, they would have repented long ago, sitting in sackcloth and ashes. ¹⁴But it will be more bearable for Tyre and Sidon at the judgment than for you. ¹⁵And you, Capernaum, will you be lifted to the heavens? No, you will go down to Hades.

¹⁶"Whoever listens to you listens to me; whoever rejects you rejects me; but whoever rejects me rejects him who sent me." ¹⁷The seventy-two returned with joy and said, "Lord, even the demons submit to us in your name."

¹⁸He replied, "I saw Satan fall like lightning from heaven. ¹⁹I have given you authority to trample on snakes and scorpions and to overcome all the power of the enemy; nothing will harm you. ²⁰However, do not rejoice that the spirits submit to you, but rejoice that your names are written in heaven."

In this last verse Jesus shows His compassion, commanding that we should not gloat even when triumphing over Satan and the fallen angels; God would have preferred that they not rebel at all. Even the archangel Michael did not curse or judge Satan; as God says, it is up to Him to judge. If we judge, we are usurping God's authority.

Because of technology, cell phones and the internet, today mankind is even more subject to temptation. Unwanted solicitations, spam, tweets, and texts, can lead us into areas that lead to evil. Texting and sexting among teens can lead to devastating consequences, bullying of decades ago is now in the form of malicious text campaigns that can so easily lead to suicide. Sexting gets out of control and internet trolls lure young and naive girls into lurid relationships and even suicide. Never before have there been so many downward spirals that masquerade as *a little bit of fun*.

Previous generations getting high on alcohol were limited by its availability and overtness of its purchase, now the pervasiveness of drugs in schools and society have a reach and cause devastation in lives that alcohol never could. Yes, alcohol can lead to addiction, but drugs lead to much more addiction and brain damage at an earlier age.

Whenever we engage in mind altering activities we open the door to the ever vigilant enemy; a crack in the door becomes a foot in the door. It is all about the mind. The enemy does not do anything physical; he works through our minds. He has no body that we can see. If we did see the demons bodies, maybe they would be so repugnant that we would simply run away from a situation. Satan can't send messages using social media, but be sure he prompts real people to do it for him. Over and over the apostles remind us to be on guard about what we allow our minds to dwell on. The first process starts when accepting Jesus as our Lord, and having the Holy Spirit enter is the renewing of our minds. By their teens the human minds are full of street wisdom, distorted truth, and outright misinformation. Those young minds have little chance to avoid the mines and traps laid by the enemy. More than ever before it is imperative that sound parental guidance comes into play. But sadly, and is it a coincidence that stable families, where parents have the time or inclination to monitor and lovingly nurture their children, is at an all-time low?

For the most part the Church, the institution and the individuals, are almost completely silent on Satan, his demons, and their tricks, deceit, and lies. The access afforded the enemy by technology, alcohol and drugs is often seen as just a social problem; of course they are, but they have a much more profound effect of eternal consequences. Without yelling messages of fire and brimstone from pulpits, congregations and seekers need to be intelligently informed. If that has no effect, some fire and brimstone could be a last resort in this world of extreme electronic games and movies; it could be more effective than we imagine. The problem with fire and brimstone is that it seems, since the onset of science fiction and horror movies starting in the 1950's and 60's, that people take messages of fire and brimstone to be as real as the movies. Even the angels helping to build the ark in the recent movie "Noah" looked more like industrial robots and the movie was more cinematic license than Bible truth.

Ultimately our bodies, and all the bodily sensations are transitory, they have built-in obsolescence. The window of opportunity is limited. It is a game where the odds are stacked against us, and Satan put the fix in before we were born, but God threw us a lifeline. When we are young time seems to move slowly, we think we will live forever, and we will have plenty of time to find out about God; time goes by faster and the clutter builds as a garage fills with stuff. There are reasons why the chances of connecting with God reduce substantially as we get older. It only takes a few words to overcome Satan and all the demons and evil in this world "Lord Jesus, I believe in what you did on the cross. I want you to be Lord of my life; help me, save me!"

Dog Days

Jasmine's hunger switch never turns off. If we are ever tempted to give in to her ever 'feed me' eyes we pay for it within half an hour. She clears the room, dogs first, women and children next; but, being master of my universe I reach for the appropriate remote and blast the highly flammable intruder into the next room.

Although she always seems hungry, she contemplates a french fry for about 5 seconds before opening the portcullis and advancing on the morsel; and morsel holder, my fingers. Like many humans she can't see what's in front of her nose, but she has a big nose, and down come the choppers with all the precision of a seagull dropping; thankfully she has a big mouth that accommodates a wide degree of error.

A few Dog Days ago I mentioned that God's economy had afforded me a newish looking Ford Escape. I thought I would give our latest chariot a little spruce up as I knew the honeymoon would soon be over. I bought some Quick Spray wax, some Armorall vinyl cleaner, and some Tire Black spray; all easy, and most importantly quick. On Saturday morning, with an uncharacteristically eager stride, I reached into the bag of cleaners and launched into action. In about 45 minutes I had 'waxed' the car. It was a lot harder to get a shine with the 'quick shine product' than I remembered, and as I placed the bottle back on a shelf, label out for easy reading, I read 'Armorall'. Good job Jasmine doesn't speak, I would never have heard the last of it.

I want you woven into a tapestry of love, in touch with everything there is to know of God. Then you will have minds confident and at rest, focused on Christ, God's great mystery.

~ Colossians 2:2 – The Message by Eugene H. Peterson

THE TAPESTRY

When we are born, we are *innocent* but broken and destined to sin. We have an inbuilt selfish nature of looking out for number one, and a desire for self-determination as provided for by our free will; mankind always strives for freedom. In our early teens we become aware, responsible for our actions. In Jewish culture when boys are 13 years old they have their bar mitzvah ceremony where they become 'men', and become 'responsible' in God's sight, but even in biblical times they were not considered mature until they were 30. We have a lifetime to consider God. When our bodies die and our spirits are released, whatever choice we have made is set.

In the western world, when we are young we think it's a time to get as much pleasure as we can; that is our priority. I was like that, extremely like that. But I think wisdom does come with age; and to me anyway, it seems the older we get the more we accept that despite knowing more, it is a smaller percentage of all there is to know. The older I get, the more I realize that what seemed like worthwhile pursuits, were often either just plain wrong, or a waste of my life. I think you can find a lot of wisdom in the Bible, just check out proverbs. It may seem simplistic at first, but don't we mess up the same way in every generation. Just look what the *pill* and drugs of the 60's gave us; a legacy of single parents, and messed up children on the streets. I look back and far from seeing it as liberating, I now see it as a time of rebelling from our parent's world of conformity to Judeo Christian social rules. Thinking then how great it was to have freedom, I now see it was taking the hand rails off a pedestrian overpass. Just asking for trouble, we got it. A word of advice about reading the Bible; read from all over, ideally all of it, not just the New Testament, not just from the gospels. Although they are a good place to start, read the Old Testament, read through what seem like boring books of the old testament, read Genesis and Exodus to see the roots of Christianity, read the books of Samuel, Kings and the prophets, and the mighty works of God, the character of God is revealed in His Bible. The Bible says to any who lack wisdom, ask and He will give it without judging them.

This is where in the next number of paragraphs I try to reveal in a more concise way the detail and extent of God's Power, Wisdom, and Love in the great plan He had from before He created the angels.

God had a plan; a plan to have servants and companions. God is like us, or should I say we are like Him. We have the emotions and drives, like pleasure and anger, love and compassion that God has. Like Him we have the desire for company. But there is a major difference. Firstly and most importantly God is Holy. Secondly God's capacity for love so far exceeds ours we are unable to fully comprehend it. God created the heavens and countless angels, and it seems they were also created in His image. He created the cosmos and man, also in large numbers; we now number seven billion. Being created with free will, both angels and mankind could go their own way, which is to ignore God. But free will was essential if His creation was to be able to love God in the way He loved it. Angels by default were *with* God. Mankind, by the corrupting work of Satan and because God is hidden from us by a *veil*, is separated from God at birth. Because of the potential of angels and mankind to want to be independent from God, He had to sort both of us, test us, to see who was absolutely for Him, and those who were not. He used Satan in heaven to provoke any angels that were not fully loyal to God to show their colours, thus sorting the angels. He used Satan and the unfaithful angels to discourage man, by any number of deceitful ways, from *seeing* God through the *veil*. The ones who do, and willingly call Jesus and God their Lord, have been separated from those who have declared, by default, that they themselves are lord of their lives.

Because God is holy, He is constrained by the rules that are part of His holiness. He cannot live in contact with sinful angels or sinful man; this would corrupt His holiness and He would no longer be holy. Satan corrupted mankind at his dawn. Angels, who already had knowledge of good and evil, were corruptible, despite being able to see God. God's mission was to separate out the angels who would sin, from those who would remain loyal and therefore not sin. Mankind was already lost, irreversibly corrupted; to be forever separated from God. God's plan was to create a door through which the separation could be overcome so mankind could reunite with God again.

God, specifically Jesus, created angels to the Father's specifications. They have had a role before the cosmos was created, probably for some extended time, from thousands to millions of years, which is inferred by the Bible. Again to the Father's specification, Jesus created the cosmos; everything there is in what seems like infinite space, including our earth. Whether it took six of our days, or unfolded in six stages, planned in detail by God, it did not create itself. For different reasons, mankind of old was correct, we, not the cosmos are the focal point of the cosmos; the rest is window dressing. The reason the rest of the cosmos is there would seem to be because it not only humbles us, but makes us wonder how such an intricate mechanism came to be, if not by a wonderful creator. Just like a delicate and intricate orchid, the nature of God is revealed in the night sky. But today, when the world needs its creator more than ever, the Hubble telescope shows us the beauty and wonder that are in God's heart; it is a gallery of His masterpieces.

Up until we were created, the angel society seemed content, even Lucifer, later to become Satan, appeared to earn and be content with accolades. Lucifer was assigned the position of Guardian Cherubim, guarding the Tree of Knowledge of Good and Evil. This post was on earth, as a special responsibility under the general *ministering to man* mandate now given to the angels. Lucifer earned his title of Satan, dragon, and serpent, when he shirked this role, being jealous of Jesus and was inwardly angered by the fact that mankind was made for Jesus' pleasure. Instead of guarding the Tree of Knowledge, Satan promoted mankind's access to it, ensuring his spiritual death and the corruption of the human race, resulting in mankind being separated from God.

Any illusions Lucifer had that mankind had been created for *him* and *his* pleasure, and even to worship *him*, were dashed, and he now spends millennia working against Jesus. Strangely, this is God's plan! God used Satan to attract the angels, who did not *love* God as He loved them, like a magnet will attract iron filings mixed with sand. God was left with holy angels. While there was a time of both the sorting of the angels and the sorting of man, the war in heaven marked the time when the angels choices became final, just as ours do when we die. Having corrupted mankind, Satan accuses mankind, before God, of having no genuine adoration of his maker, while at the same time convincing more and more angels of his philosophy that promotes the freedom for angels; out from under God's authority. Going along with Satan's desires to prove his accusations, Satan tested God's apparently faithful human servants, such as Job. All the time God was playing Satan, who was unaware he was being used to *sort* mankind. God actively uses Satan to sort us; to make it clear by our actions, those who seek after and find God, who believe they are loved by Him and want to return that love. This is part of God's plan from before He even created angels. He knew Lucifer would turn against Him given the right circumstances. When God was sure all the angels had chosen sides, and all of the rebellious angels had effectively made their positions public, He waited for Jesus, who had been born and grown to an age where what he said counted (considered to have been achieved at the age of 30), to complete His three year ministry. His plan then called for Jesus to be sacrificed.

Satan thought he had succeeded in getting rid of Jesus, leaving mankind still corrupted. Satan had been dogging Jesus since his birth, and before he could clap his hands with joy at the crucifixion, he realized that at the last moment God the Father had played him. All of a sudden he realized that God the Father had placed the totality of the sins of mankind on Jesus making Him pay the penalty required by God's justice. In doing this Jesus, the perfect sacrifice, acted as the 'scapegoat', paid the penalty required by Holy justice. God's holiness demands that sins be punished; a penalty must be paid. Jesus, having taken on the sins of man, paid the penalty at His death; this was the real pain that Jesus suffered, even though to us it is the lashings that make us squirm. How can we understand the pain of this atonement? There must have been an almost unbearable anguish as God the Father had to separate Himself from Jesus for the first time in Their existence, as Jesus had become sinful. This completely and irreversibly undoes the total corrupting work of Satan, and mankind is free to accept this work of salvation and be with God when his spirit is freed from his human body. The game is over, the angels are sorted, but now as the population on earth increases exponentially God casts Satan and his angels to earth for the next stage of His plan.

Satan is no longer accusing man, promoting rebellion, the rebellion has failed. There was war in heaven and Satan lost. Now just as God used Satan in heaven as a polarizing influence, God being the other pole, He does the same on earth. Now Satan and the fallen angels, hidden from direct view by humans, use every ounce of their guile and intrigue to prevent mankind from finding and being useful to God. Satan is a master strategist, the most subtle of liars, and has guided the evolution of the world cultures, to be the theatre of his grand illusions. Satan has been played in God's plan, sorting the angels, exposing those not completely faithful to God, and now is being played to sort man. As with angels, when the time is right, God will call a halt to Satan's activities, and will confront all His human and angelic enemies on earth in the final showdown.

Led by Jesus, God's heavenly armies will witness the fall of Satan's armies by the Word of Jesus alone. The triumph will be celebrated in a banquet where Jesus, as the bridegroom, welcomes His bride the Church, the faithful of mankind, written in the Lamb's Book of Life (Jesus is the Lamb), since before the earth was created. Faithful mankind and faithful angels will now be together to worship their Creator, and to enjoy each other's company in whatever God has in mind.

Finally at Pentecost, just after Jesus crucifixion, the Holy Spirit came to live with those who believe in Jesus and His work of salvation, His Spirit a companion Spirit with ours. In this way God is always with those who call Him Lord. From that point on mankind has been living in the age of grace, our sins cancelled by the atoning work of Jesus.

Grace is what makes Christianity different from any other religion, including Judaism. Grace allows us to sin and still be right with God; the sin has already been paid for, God's justice has been satisfied. However that does not mean there are not consequences. There is man's justice to satisfy, and God's plan to make us more like Jesus. He may discipline us as He says He will do to all those He loves, as we do to our children. This may result in us going through more learning curves; usually something less than enjoyable. God may withhold blessings, just as we would not reward bad behavior in our children. Grace is not a license to sin. If we take it that way, I imagine God will crank up the discipline until we get the message; don't underestimate the power of conscience or guilt. Neither makes us *un-right* with God; the Holy Spirit speaks through our conscience and through other ways. Guilt is a natural response when we do something that is against our heart beliefs. Asking forgiveness from God is the fix in case of guilt, but in the process of talking with Him, it is amazing what else transpires; try it!

We are so privileged to live in the age of grace, the Mosaic Law and its sacrificial requirements were such a burden. That is why it is said that Jesus has set us *free!* We are free to make mistakes, to stumble in our walk with Jesus; we do not lose our salvation. There are no prayers that we *have* to pray, no rules that we *have* to follow. Of course God wants us to be guided by the Holy Spirit inside us, and to read His word, so that we grow in an understanding of Him, while renewing our minds, so that we become more and more like Jesus. Being a Christian, opposite to the *street* view, is the most freeing of lifestyles! No wonder Jesus says He wants us "To lead an abundant life." That does not mean we will not face the trials of this world like anybody else. God may bless us so life is more enjoyable on the whole, but there are evil people and demons out there just waiting to give us a bad day. On top of that remember, Satan, through other people, may persecute you; not in the *west* too much, but in some other countries you can be jailed, tortured, and even put to death for just being a Christian or talking about Christianity. Still in all situations, Jesus, through the Holy Spirit gives you a *peace that passes understanding*. This is real; I have experienced this in the dire situations.

God's overall sifting process for angels and mankind is simplistically elegant. It was like a sloping battlefield, God was at the bottom with the angels, the angels had to make an effort to desert God for Satan, who was at the top of the slope. There could be no mistake; the evidence was in their actions. For man, it was the opposite, we were already corrupted, sinners; God knew that Satan would see to that. We were at the bottom of the slope, but because we were separated from God, He was at the top. Jesus had paid for our sins, but we had to accept it, by seeking God, by climbing up the slope and making Jesus Lord of our lives. Satan is all over the slope, trying with unending strategies to stop us, and then hindering our walk with Jesus after we have accepted Him. We do not have to clean up our lives, but we do have to clearly choose to surrender to the authority of Jesus, and through Him God. The evidence is in our actions.

I think our lives are the time God gives us, in a very constrained environment, to make a choice, for Him or against Him. I think the constrained environment intentionally prevents us from seeing the other realms of heaven; seeing God or Satan directly. We have to decide based on the influences from each. It seems God has made it harder for us than He has the angels; they just had to remain loyal. We have to search for and then purposefully accept Jesus as Lord but Jesus has done a lot more for us than He did for the angels; He died for us. Before Jesus, God had His prophets, and His anointed people. Jesus came in human form, performed miracles, as God the Father directed, and left the *church of believers*, His Church, as His earthly legacy. Satan was *cast down to earth* with his angels and does his best to keep humans, by any means possible, away from God. He does not waste his time on those just hell bent on getting the most out of *their* lives on this earth. Those he doesn't have to worry about as they are by default his. But as he is on a mission, he focuses on those he sees as enemies and potential enemies.

Another thing to understand is the reason this whole war started. Satan despised being God's servant, having to minister to humans, being the Guardian Cherubim in the

Garden of Eden, guarding the Tree of the Knowledge of Good and Evil. The war started because God created humans with free will, and wanted a relationship, where the love He had for His creation was reciprocated. The plan where He would use angels to facilitate the development of this relationship could not fail. Satan was played from the very beginning. Satan was irritated by God's plan to the point of fomenting unrest in the community of angels, which eventually led to war.

God knew this would happen. It was also a process to sift the angels; to see who would remain loyal to Him. He also knew that only one third would oppose Him; He knew He would win. So now God has cleaned house, cast all the opposition down to earth and locked up those who would interfere with the next part of the plan. In casting them down to earth He changed them into loveless beings and limited their powers in a way that served His purposes. Notice that, even with Job, Satan had to ask for permission to go against him, first with his wealth and family, then with extra permission, Job's health.

This period since the war in heaven, must be a continuing hell for Satan. His plan to prevent Jesus being born was thwarted every step of the way. Satan, not being able to see into the future and only be in one place at a time, had no more clue than Herod about the real role of Jesus when He was born. Satan was instrumental in the crucifixion of Jesus, manipulating the Sanhedrin and the crowd that called for His death. Satan's plan was to at least get rid of Jesus from earth, and to foil whatever God was up to. He knew that as with all spirits, Jesus could not be *really* killed, annihilated; getting rid of Jesus-human was his best option. Instead of succeeding in even this, God had played him again and actually ensured the culmination of God's plan for Jesus walking our earth.

Jesus gained credibility by His ministry of three years. He demonstrated God's love to the people, and His miracles proved He was God. He then paid the penalty that God the Father required to free mankind from Satan's blight, because the Father is bound by His own justice. The penalty had to be paid so that we, in our sin strewn lives, may be made holy and presentable to God the Father, who is holy and cannot have sin in His presence. Jesus paid the penalty, He provided for our salvation. It is His gift and we cannot earn it nor improve upon it by our works. We can't make ourselves holy, it is the only way to become His children, have a loving relationship, and be in His presence. He made us in His image. He is Spirit, we are spirit, but He trapped us in these bodies of matter, and limited us to see only this Earthly environment to give us a period where those, who yearn to fill that void He made inside us, could fill it.

Earth is a convenient classroom. God provided a perfect place, to sense Him, through the craftsmanship of this world, and His cosmos. But as with Abraham, He also reaches out; Genesis is really worth reading! He wants us to seek Him, really seek Him, get to know Him, trust Him, and rely on Him and not ourselves. He wants us to realize we are *spirit*, made in His image, and to become His children, despite being corrupt at birth. If we seek Him out, if we have faith in Jesus, and accept that His death on the cross really did clean our slate, and make Him Lord of our lives, then we will become joint heirs with Jesus, the son of God the Father, being adopted into His family as His children, and live forever with Him.

Currently there is the earth with a spiritual realm overlaid onto it, and then there is God's heaven. Since the crucifixion the fallen angels don't have access to God's heaven. I think it is a wholly separate realm with an impenetrable wall, like the chasm that will exist for all who have rejected God.

Everything that Jesus has said of heaven has always been in the superlative. It is wondrously beyond our imagination. Earth is a prison to limit our knowledge and experience of the spiritual realms. We are spirit, created in God's image with His character, doubly imprisoned, firstly in a body and secondly in a realm constricted by time and space; a material place. Luckily God arranged our DNA so that our body prisons expire, but it is not so much a prison as a classroom. The classroom is our world, our earth, and even beyond, the cosmos. God has left His finger prints all over the cosmos in the way He set nature in motion. Initially He did this to make us wonder at its scope and power, as we did not understand its science, but later to make us wonder at the incredible complexity such as our own DNA. We are unique, each of us. All living things from slime to humans are defined by a DNA language. The way we have chosen to read it, it has an alphabet of only four letters and has the equivalent of words, sentences, paragraphs and books. It would take about a thousand books in the DNA language of God to define a human, with only about the last twenty of those books used to define our differences, race to race and person to person.

A Tapestry is like a huge carpet and in medieval times was used to memorialize great events. The Bayeux tapestry is not really a tapestry because it is embroidered on linen with brilliant woolen yarns rather than woven, is 230 feet long and 20 inches high. It commemorates the battle of Hastings in England in 1066. It was created in Kent, England, after being commissioned by Bishop Odo, William the Conqueror's half-brother, in the 1070's. It depicts scenes leading up to the Norman conquest of England, by William, Duke of Normandy. Harold, Earl of Wessex, who became King of England, was defeated at the battle of Hastings where he suffered an archer's arrow to the eye. It currently resides in the Bayeux Tapestry Museum in Bayeux, Normandy, France, but a Victorian replica is housed in the Reading Museum, near London, England. It is a marvelous tapestry with over 30 scenes in sets depicting the Journey to Normandy, The Prisoner, The Mysterious Lady, Brothers in Arms, The Oath, The Return, The King is Dead, …Long Live The King, Planning the Invasion, The Crossing, Beachhead, William Rides to War, and finally The Battle of Hastings.

If that was a tapestry depicting a rather short series of events a thousand years ago with woolen yarns, imagine a tapestry that could be created of the dramatic and climatic events of the events in God's plan, especially with the fabulous colours and metallic threads of today. The tapestry I imagine is a picture-history in which every detail of the stories, linkages and players, from angels to the new heaven and new earth that God promises, are woven so that each person's life is portrayed by threads. Everything is visible, no invisible realms. It is a picture representing events and relationships, but just like a medieval tapestry it tells a story over time from left to right. There are large blank spaces at the left and right ends, they are the parts of God's story that we cannot know right now, times infinitely in the past, and infinitely in the future. Just like the Bayeux Tapestry it has sets of scenes:

Angels

Suddenly the tapestry blazes with colour as God creates angels and decorates heaven as a dwelling place. He is at the centre of His heaven, there is only His heaven. It is bright, brilliantly bright; the threads are like jewels, they sparkle with every colour and hue. There are solid threads of gold and silver, and transparent threads of sapphire, emerald and ruby.

Creation

Semi-formed images take shape, the nebulas of our cosmos like clusters of orchids, some of the flowers He will create later. The tapestry is now an extravagant sequence of scenes depicted in violent colour in the transition from God's wondrous heaven, through a developing cosmos of unimaginable beauty, to that of a developed cosmos. Then comes our earth, land and seas, brilliant flowers, some tiny alpine flowers, others brilliant tropical show-offs waiting to compete with equally show-off parrots, shrubs and trees of all shapes and sizes against a sky of pale sapphire and animals of all shapes and sizes, even some that seem to make no sense.

Man

There is man and woman; the picture is one of wonder and delight. They walk naked, bronze bodies silhouetted against lush vegetation, waterfalls, springs, and ponds. It is idyllic, at peace with all forms of animals and birds sharing their world unafraid.

The Fall

The man and woman change, they now appear clothed in animal skins the animals keep their distance. In the background is a brilliant angel flashing a great sword. The first threads of black appear in heaven, it is the seed of dissention born by the free will of Lucifer. It grows, and creates more seeds as it spreads like cancer through the heavenly host. It grows like weeds, like thorns with golden spikes, and beautiful thistles, with purple flowers, but covered in tiny silver spikes, threads of black weaving but not overcoming the brilliant beings God has created. Even then God had His threads, invisible like glass, from Him to Lucifer, like puppet strings. Lucifer was and will always be God's servant. Through Lucifer, God allowed the angels to be sorted and refined.

The Tapestry

Satan's web captures angels

Those who had within them the essence of rebellion were attracted to Lucifer and the web of promises he spun, like a web of silk and diamonds glittering in the light he reflected from God. Lucifer captures the unwitting angels as he spins his web of deceit, controlling them like puppets himself.

Cast out of Heaven

When the time was right and all those who would rebel had chosen their side, God exiled them to another spiritual realm outside of His heaven, one overlaying the earth, which He had created along with the cosmos. He commanded His loyal servant angels to eject the rebel angels into the spiritual realm that shares its existence with earth; there is lightning, and a great star falling to earth. Lush earth with a myriad of plants and trees expressing their exuberance in colour is marred by patches of black fog and the webs of black silk and diamonds.

The first sifting of Man

Corrupted mankind is woven in drab threads. He does not reflect the light of God, except for one man who emerges from the multitude in bronze thread, coming through a rainbow arc with all of God's innocent creation. Blacks and greys of storm give way to brilliant yellows and gold of sunshine, there are whites, blues, silver and gold threads, and a dove with an olive twig. Mankind starts again.

Satan accuses faithful Mankind

The picture morphs into an enormous battlefield stretching through millennia. It is filled with mankind; hovering over one side is Satan, a monstrous dragon, green with envy and huge angry eyes of red, only a shell of the once brilliant Lucifer. On the other side is God, blazing in glory, even the thread radiates. Between Satan and the bedazzled humans are his demons, like every hideous creature imaginable and worse, from huge slimy toads to fearful warriors, their eyes, devoid of love and compassion, stare red with purposeful intent.

Son of Man and Son of God

Between God and mankind, is Jesus, in blazing silver and gold thread. He commands the angels, in brilliant white robes with silver and gold sashes, to roll out the plan of God the Father, like a ribbon of glass with gold writing, over the millennia. The will of God is carried out by God's angels coming and going from His presence, on paths of clouds with golden ladders and chariots of fire reaching from God to earth. Unwittingly, Satan does God's bidding through puppet strings woven with transparent silk to the dragon which, in turn has puppet strings to his demons.

Salvation

Soldiers stand around uninterested. Others throw dice for a garment. Jesus hangs on a cross in silhouette His head slumped, with blood running from His side. He wears the gold crown of victory. Suddenly the skies, in black with jagged streaks of lightning in silver, turn the afternoon eerie and ominous. The dark skies give way to brilliant sunlight, as Jesus ascends to the Father seated on His throne. The scene is brilliant with golds, silver and bronze glittering metallic threads. Angels lay prostrate around the throne, row after row of angels.

The Age of Grace

So beautiful a phrase, and so luxurious is the scenery of the background, but so horrible is the depiction. This scene is wide; it is a battleground with many sub-scenes. It shows the last few thousand years of the life of man, almost everything is corrupted. On the side closest to Satan it is all shades of grey, some of the men have knives stabbing others in the back, as they climb up half broken ladders; demons pull at the men on the ladders and men are falling off. The ladders lead up to different levels, with bigger cars and houses the higher you go, others with lifelines from God's side are helping those who have fallen to the ground. Luke-warmers are almost transparent, ghosts, in the middle and wear religious hats, unaware of the battle being fought. Jesus casts a brilliant light over this battle. Men and angels reflect this light but the demons there cover their eyes. The demons dig traps, change sign posts, but are kept from the men by powerful angels with flashing swords. Angels carry nourishment from God's storehouse for body, mind and spirit for those who bear God's mark.

The final battle

The scene changes from a battlefield where the battle lines are blurred, to one where Satan's generals and the souls won by him stand opposed to Jesus and His angel armies, as in times of old. The clean orderly lines give way to a vast area of ragged red strands; a sea of blood and agony.

The wedding Banquet

Like some oversized Greek amphitheatre in brilliant white marble; the scene recedes into the distance with perspective without losing its form. It is the banquet of the reunion, the wedding feast of the Lamb, a reunion between God and those who have answered God's call to join Him through the salvation of Jesus. Jesus is the banquet's host and God's glory lights the whole enormous place, which seems to go on forever. Everyone is dressed in white robes, and there is endless praise with great joy. The Saints wear white robes with silver and gold sashes, they mingle with angels, and there are so many the scene is brilliant in whites, silver and gold and transparent threads like glass; elaborate tables are decked with colourful fruit and wine.

New Heaven and New Earth

Still with bright colours and gold and silver threads, the image of the feast fades as the tapestry moves into the future with the new heaven and new earth, with the New Jerusalem described in gold and jewels. There is a great expanse of cloth waiting to be embroidered. It goes on forever, and is waiting on God to speak the tapestry into existence.

Sometimes words speak louder than images. In his early adult years my son wrote some worship music. With great attention to detail he played and sang with others and recorded his songs and those of others onto a CD. It seems, when I play it, that he captured the very essence of the image of God. He sings and plays with a variety of young ladies, all very harmonious and exuding life. Early adult hood seems to refine the exuberance of youth without losing the creative quality. The songs span a range of contemporary style music from deep to playful, but all seem in harmony with the real and loving God, who I can imagine to be invigorating that vibrancy with His very being. If I close my eyes, I can imagine the amphitheatre, the banquet of the Lamb.

He created us to live with Him, closely, to engage and enjoy us and we Him.

If we are amazed, constrained in these human bodies, at the wonders of this world, just imagine how totally fulfilling it would be without the constraints as joint heirs with Jesus in His realms. Words cannot describe the wonders, joy, and peace we will experience in His realm, as His children.

Dog Days

When I was in my late 30's all of a sudden I found that I had lost the distinction between good and bad things that happened to me. It's not that they went away, or stopped happening, it's that my perspective had changed.

One New Year's Eve my wife failed to negotiate the turn into our driveway. The old Beetle decided it wanted a rest in the ditch. My wife walked the hundred yards of laneway to our century old house. I had been working a lot in Ottawa but had the next day off; it would make a nice rest. She opened the door, almost in tears. She told me what had happened just a few minutes before, and I responded "oh well, I'll get it out in the morning." My response surprised both of us. I was an uptight AA type. I comforted her and said it would all be good by the time we needed the car again. I walked down the lane and calmly tried to assess the situation as I sat in the ditch full of snow in the dark. I pondered my new found calmness about something that would have normally ruined my day in my previous life. Had I become just an A type personality?

I can't remember how I got it out, but I know it took a good part of my New Year's Day off. That was my transformation from viewing events as good or bad, but seeing them as just events. From then on I decided not to judge events, not to categorize them. How could I tell if God was using them to change me? If God had brought it about, it must be good. Who was I to label it; wasn't He renewing my mind?

I saw the Holy City, the New Jerusalem, coming down out of heaven from God, prepared as a bride beautifully dressed for her husband.

~ Revelation 21:2

BOOKENDS

Bookends was intended to be some musings on what could have gone on before the age of mankind on earth and after the final battle, although its somewhat of an exaggeration to call it a battle. All the forces, in the hundreds of millions coming against Jerusalem, but really against God, are wiped out merely by the Word of Jesus, His double edged sword, and the blood runs deep.

Revelation Chapter 19

[11] I saw heaven standing open and there before me was a white horse, whose rider is called Faithful and True. With justice he judges and wages war. [12] His eyes are like blazing fire, and on his head are many crowns. He has a name written on him that no one knows but he himself. [13] He is dressed in a robe dipped in blood, and his name is the Word of God. [14] The armies of heaven were following him, riding on white horses and dressed in fine linen, white and clean. [15] Coming out of his mouth is a sharp sword with which to strike down the nations. "He will rule them with an iron scepter." He treads the winepress of the fury of the wrath of God Almighty. [16] On his robe and on his thigh he has this name written:

KING OF KINGS AND LORD OF LORDS.

17And I saw an angel standing in the sun, who cried in a loud voice to all the birds flying in midair, "Come, gather together for the great supper of God, 18so that you may eat the flesh of kings, generals, and the mighty, of horses and their riders, and the flesh of all people, free and slave, great and small."

19Then I saw the beast and the kings of the earth and their armies gathered together to wage war against the rider on the horse and his army. 20But the beast was captured, and with it the false prophet who had performed the signs on its behalf. With these signs he had deluded those who had received the mark of the beast and worshiped its image. The two of them were thrown alive into the fiery lake of burning sulfur. 21The rest were killed with the sword coming out of the mouth of the rider on the horse, and all the birds gorged themselves on their flesh.

More metaphorically, it is described in an earlier chapter.

Revelation Chapter 14

14I looked, and there before me was a white cloud, and seated on the cloud was one like a son of man with a crown of gold on his head and a sharp sickle in his hand. 15Then another angel came out of the temple and called in a loud voice to him who was sitting on the cloud, "Take your sickle and reap, because the time to reap has come, for the harvest of the earth is ripe." 16So he who was seated on the cloud swung his sickle over the earth, and the earth was harvested.

¹⁷Another angel came out of the temple in heaven, and he too had a sharp sickle. ¹⁸Still another angel, who had charge of the fire, came from the altar and called in a loud voice to him who had the sharp sickle, "Take your sharp sickle and gather the clusters of grapes from the earth's vine, because its grapes are ripe." ¹⁹The angel swung his sickle on the earth, gathered its grapes and threw them into the great winepress of God's wrath. ²⁰They were trampled in the winepress outside the city, and blood flowed out of the press, rising as high as the horses' bridles for a distance of 1,600 stadia.

1,600 stadia is 180 miles or 300 kms. Strange the way a metaphor is mixed with explicit heights and distances, except to describe the enormity in numbers of those who opposed God. Revelation is an amazing book, the last in the Bible, and in the early Chapters gives warnings to the various ages of the churches, described by the name of real churches. These were established by the early Christians, but in Revelation, each also parallels the nature of the Church in sequential ages. The later Chapters recount the plagues that will be poured out on the earthly population, proud, independent and shaking their fist at God until the end. The final Chapters describe a new earth, where God lives on earth with man. Whether this earth is still part of the cosmos or a metaphor for a combined heaven and earth in a new form, who knows, as the bodies of the faithful among mankind have been given glorified bodies, such as the angels had when manifested on earth.

There is a thousand year period where Satan is chained up. He is released for a short time to either test the faithfulness of the angels and man, or to prove, as required by God's justice, that he has been totally wrong all along, and soon meets the fate of the beast and his false prophet. They had been thrown into the lake of fire a thousand years earlier.

The New Jerusalem is described in such great detail, and so metaphorical, but with explicit measurements, that it seems it could be a description of a reality that we cannot comprehend and written with the words of John the apostle's time. Revelation is so stunning in warning, in dread, in finality, and in promise, that it has to be read; even if you are not a believer.

What came before is a complete mystery, as there is no evidence of it except that Satan had a track record of 'blamelessness'. There are only angels and God. There are 'creatures' in heaven, but I assume these are classes of angels, as are the cherubim. As for what comes next, God has shown no evidence of ever being idle. On the contrary, He has shown Himself to be a very active and creative God. The physical cosmos, although a fascinating place for us, is very 'old hat' for God. Its purpose to constrain us within a place bound by time and space, making the other heavens invisible to us in order that we must seek Him to find Him, is over. We could spend a long time satisfying our curiosity about it, and maybe that will be an opportunity in the thousand years, but I think the time of the earth as we know it, and even the other heavens, will be over by the time we are at Christ's wedding banquet, but there are powerful hints of 'ruling cities', that cannot be ignored. God is too big and too creative to exist with us for eternity without wanting to create even greater things.

Dog Days

The forest is bordered by an upmarket neighbourhood and the closest house to where the trail starts has a large ornamental pond. Did I mention Jasmine loves the water? After she enjoyed a cooling off in this pond, following a walk on a hot summer's day last year I keep her on the leash within about 100ft of the car. We walk from the car up the rise and out of smell shot of the pond, and then it's treat time. Placid up until that point she sits and drools while I fumble for a dog biscuit. While she gives the treat a crunch and a swallow, I unhook the leash; I reverse the process on the way back. From that point for the whole walk until back in the car she is focused; she is on a smell mission. She has to put out every smoldering smelly landmine. Like Satan's landmines they are invisible, but the combination of her smelly landmine detector and millisecond squirt control, makes her an effective landmine neutralizer. She gets a treat when we turn around as a reminder I have treats, whereupon the mission changes to litter control. Litter is in the form of dead sticks dropped by the careless trees since her last walk. There being no litter bins on the path, she dedicatedly eats the sticks.

I always have a treat available in case she decides to check out the houses back over the rise for litter (or other dogs' breakfasts). My shouts of 'Treat, treat, Jazzbag treat" always work within the latency time between her ears and her treat brain cell; it's never more than 8 seconds after she has disappeared over the rise. I'm more in the range of 8 days after I disappear after some worldly tinsel litter.

All Scripture is God-breathed and is useful for teaching, rebuking, correcting and training in righteousness.

~ 2 Timothy 3:16

ASSUMPTIONS

If you allow too many variables when trying to see a pattern, you are faced with too many alternatives, and as they say you can't see the forest for the trees. Our minds, my mind at least, can only handle a few variables; even a few variables seem to spawn endless possibilities. It's like trying to predict the ultimate pattern of a tree's roots from the few main roots that are evident at the surface. For the purpose of limiting the possibilities, and to have any chance at analysis I have reduced the variables by making certain assumptions. These are basic Christian tenents: firstly, the God of the Bible is all-knowing, all-seeing, and all-powerful, able to do literally anything, and possesses limitless love. Secondly, the Bible is true, all of it. If something doesn't make sense to me, it just means I don't understand it fully. I believe God's ways are best, and to follow them brings me good; not that I am able to follow them that well. Thirdly God created the human race for His pleasure, and it is His desire to have a relationship with us and, one day, for us to live with Him.

I use the term God for the three in one God of the Christian faith. This triune God consists of three distinct entities: God the Father, Jesus, who always was, but whose spirit was bound in human form when He came to earth as a baby to fulfill part of God's plan, and finally the Holy Spirit. The three act as one, with one purpose, unfolding the will of God the Father. Even if you do not hold to these assumptions, read on, seeing a bigger picture may change your mind. I hope that in seeing the big picture, God's grand plan to strain the sheep from the goats through the sieve of life on this earth, that you will gain confidence in the Bible itself. I can attest to the Bible seeming to be alive when I read it. Through the working of the Holy Spirit within me, the same passage seems to speak differently to me each time I read it. Small things I don't remember seeing before, even though I may have read them a hundred times jump out and have their say in a meaningful way in my life at that moment.

Although the Bible was written by a number of people, it is widely believed that they were inspired by God to write what they did; in fact the Bible says that about itself. Much of the Old Testament is the history of the Israelites, who became our current-day Jews, and a collection of books written by a series of prophets and kings. Israelites are the descendants of Jacob (a descendant of Abraham, through Isaac). God renamed Jacob *Israel*, and the twelve tribes were named after the sons of Jacob. Joseph, one of Jacob's sons had two sons and they were the patriarchs of two half tribes. The prophets were anointed with the Holy Spirit, allowing a direct communication with God, which they relayed as guidance, warnings, and prophesy, to the people of Israel. Moses gave the people the basis of the Old Testament in the Septuagint, the first five books of the Old Testament, and there are some books of profound wisdom, namely the Psalms, Proverbs, Ecclesiastes and others. The New Testament contains the accounts of four of Jesus' companions during His ministry on earth: Matthew, Mark, Luke, and John. It includes a record of the early church in the book of Acts, letters by Paul, who initially persecuted Christians, but became one of Jesus' most active disciples, a number of other letters, and lastly John the apostle's account of a revelation of the future given to him while in exile on the island of Patmos.

Jesus' ministry started when He was 30 and ended when he was crucified at the age of 33. Our global dating system takes the year of Jesus birth as year zero. At Pentecost, an incident 40 days after the resurrection of Jesus, all those who believed in Jesus and believed in what He had done were anointed with the Holy Spirit, heralding the current age of grace. This age of grace was established by Jesus taking on the sins of the world, past, present, and future, and paying the penalty to satisfy God's justice. This makes us right with God, regardless of our past, present and future sins, as long as we accept what Jesus did.

The majority of the dots that are used to construct the dot-picture for this book, the framework of the big picture plan, are taken from the Old Testament, with a few long lines to dots in the New Testament and Revelation. Lines can also be extrapolated into less clear times before and after the existence of this earth.

 Dog Days

It is interesting that mankind and angels seem to be the only beings capable of pride. Jazz, like all animals, seems to be quite hard wired, with a degree of freedom that they primarily use to find food and procreate. Their behavior is modified by circumstances and environment, but they never, ever seem to exhibit pride. Even a strutting cock only seems to strut because he is hard wired. Humans, particularly in the west see a lack of pride, or lack of self-esteem, as we relabel it, as not normal. We do our best to foster at least a modicum of pride. Pride in others, like children, is akin to respect and regard, and distinct from pride in self.

Pride seems to go along with capability, but not always. Pride is like a persistent stain; we can hide it, or ignore it, but that is as genuine as the mask many of us wear on a Sunday at church.

Some people are genuine; they are accomplished, heads and shoulders above others, but are meek, as if they do not hold their talent in high regard. When we stand in the company of God, pride is an ugly characteristic. Jazz makes no apology for her lack of talent; her bright beady eyes in her expressionless face merely say 'love me'. Her cheeky look, while she does a 'snatch and dash' with a slipper, right between our legs, is the same except her tail is upright, and wags triumphantly. Maybe pride is part of the fall of man and maybe one of the more significant issues. We should not take what Jesus said about this lightly; "the meek shall inherit the earth." His statements like this litter the New Testament.

My sheep listen to my voice; I know them, and they follow me.

~ John 10:27

IF I WERE GOD

We've almost all thought it, if not said it. We have a very simplistic view of our world and its social structures and cultures. Most of our plans to run the world would only work in an extreme dictatorship. Opinions voiced so easily "If I were God I would not allow war." Oh yeah, how? Passing global laws doesn't work; laws need to be enforced. We have many laws, and many international agreements. The problem is human nature. We lie, cheat, and ignore what we have agreed to, collectively or individually. The chances of a marriage working are about 50%, and we make a big fuss about those agreements. Put yourself in God's place and try to steer people to do anything that does not benefit them directly at a superficial level, while allowing them free will. We were made in the image of God. God has free will; He does not violate ours.

That is the fundamental problem with God's plan to create beings He can love and be loved by. We are torn between what we feel in our guts at a time of reflection, when we can sense that higher power calling us, and the tinsel that shines bright in our eyes, the tinsel that provokes our most basic desires. Under the right circumstances we display many of the characteristics of Jesus when He walked this earth. Most of the time however we are guided, if not driven, by basic instincts and rushing hormones, urged on in a sea of clever advertising to satisfy our self-centered nature. We see it in our own children, influenced by peers and advertising. It's very hard to get them to understand the transient nature of fashions and fads and to save their money for something more worthwhile. And that's just the innocent stuff. Currently, the news reports that way over 50% of people think it's acceptable to cheat on exams and tax returns. Is free will the fundamental problem with God's plan and the problem with our trying to show a better path for our children? Maybe it's not a problem; maybe it's essential for the children God wants as heirs. Maybe Satan's the problem and the ten cents he keeps sticking in? We could be more autocratic and deny our children their freedom of choice, to tightly control their money, where they go, who they meet. But few of us would find that satisfying, and it's probably a quick way to lose the respect and love of our children; doesn't sound like a good way for God to reach us either.

Being God has its challenges if we do not violate free will. Zapping Hitler into oblivion, as soon as he started to be evil, is pretty much the ultimate violation of his free will. Free will is a major problem!

With this in mind, is there any world issue you have a solution for? If you're a parent, I would be surprised if you haven't resorted to the words "Because I said so." These are probably the most frustrating words we can utter, for us and for our children. The words say you have failed at every level, to us, and to our children. Would you rather have robots? They would do what they are told, but it would kind of take the fun out of family and raising children. We have fun when they have fun. We melt when they even casually remark "Love you." God created us for His pleasure; the same reason you had children, though you may describe it in other words.

It seems almost every culture in the world reveres some higher entity, as far back as almost any culture can remember they had a god or gods. Even as youngsters, we grasp the basic concept and we are comfortable with it. They are all perceived to have great power and influence in the lives of man, including after we die. Besides not being willing to violate our free will, God has another problem in getting us to accept His direction; He is governed by His own justice. If your children go against your wishes, even direct instruction, do you ground them for life? You may feel like issuing that edict, but even if you do, you later relent to a more proportional punishment. God says He disciplines those He loves. There are many parallels between us and God. God says He made us in His image; doesn't sound too farfetched when you look at some of our shared characteristics.

So here we have it. God created us for His pleasure, like parents have children, even though He doesn't share the same physical realm as His human creations. We don't share our babies' cribs either. He wants to develop a relationship with us. The angels in heaven rejoice when even one of us is reconciled to Him, that is, when we are saved from eternal separation from Him when our bodies die.

What would children have to do before their parents would cast them off? What if they rebelled and the children cast off their parents? Think of a situation where the children are in boarding school, or are off at summer camp. You are busy travelling on business non-stop, but make every effort to stay in touch, to guide them as they grow. At some point school must end, summer camp ends and the busses assemble to take the children home. Have your children grown so independent, they think they know it all? Could they refuse to actually come home, wanting to go off and do their own thing? Mark Twain once remarked "When I was ten, I thought my parents knew everything. When I became twenty, I was convinced they knew nothing. Then, at thirty, I realized I was right when I was ten."

Seems mankind has a similar attitude about God. Six thousand years ago, and for thousands of years after, we gave God credit for a lot more than we do today. Then we got clever a thousand years ago and started to work out our place in the universe, and as the centuries progressed we haven't so much elevated ourselves as usurped God's lordship. As the human species has *grown up* we have seen God as less and less relevant, but maybe that is starting to reverse, as with Mark Twain's remark. Have we at last come full circle, and arrived at a point where we have peeled back the secrets of the universe just enough to see elegant harmony, balance, and order?

Dog Days

Jasmine has a thing about slippers, boots, or almost any of our footwear. It seems that in times of joy and in times of sorrow (both for her) she will trot off and bring us various items of footwear. A theatrical whack on the head is preceded with a theatrical clenching shut of her eyes, followed by a wag of her tail.

We tried every element of negative and positive reinforcement we could think of to break the habit and convince her that was BAD. Jasmine is a hand-me-down dog, she did not wag her tail for months, she makes no sound as communication with us, and only responds to a few words, despite presumably having a large brain (or brain cavity - the jury is still out). She is always in need of cuddles and rubs, rarely giving anything in return.

The other night for some strange reason I remembered back to my childhood, sometime when I was around the age of 5. I remember being a pest and doing something to upset my mum. She must have been stressed, and shouted at me, this distressed me greatly and I remember saying, "You don't love me anymore", that concept being the reason for my distress. Now as psychological punishment we have simply been putting Jasmine in her cage with no toys and ignoring her when she plays the game. Silently her eyes sob '"Don't you love me anymore?" She reacted to the new strategy immediately, and the footwear game is dying a death. Did I mention she doesn't seem to have a very good memory!

"For I know the plans I have for you," declares the LORD,
*"plans to prosper you and not to harm you,
plans to give you hope and a future."*

~ Jeremiah 29:11

CREATING A NATION GOD'S WAY

This book reveals that God's plan all along is to create beings for His pleasure. That pleasure is love based; He wants to have a close relationship with them, angels and man. He wants to live in close proximity with them, love them as a Father, and be loved by them. God is Holy, and as such cannot *live* with evil. We need to be Holy to *live* with God. God is Just; He is constrained by it and if He were not or existed outside of Justice He would cease to be a Holy God or even God at all! For those who die in rebellion against God, His justice demands that they be separated from Him forever. Those who do not rebel but fail to heed His guidance get disciplined in this life. Not only do we suffer the consequences of our actions, "please God don't let him give me a ticket, I will never speed again" prayers are pointless, but He also arranges more constructive events in our lives. His plan of guiding events inherently has parallels of justice and discipline.

Abraham

The fact that we are far from holy is obvious. It has probably always been the same, but we covered it with a veneer of civility for a few thousand years. It seems that started to fall apart in the sixties and was fully exposed by the arrival of the 21st century. At the time of Abraham, nations in the Middle

East had a variety of gods. Some of these called for child sacrifice and parents would place their babies into the cupped hands of a large cast image of their god; the hands had been heated to a tremendous temperature by a fire set below them and the baby burned to death. No wonder God's plan for His nation was to replace the nations that currently lived in the Promised Land'.

God needed to raise up a holy nation that would show the world how to be holy. The story of Abraham, the common starting point for Jews, Christians, and Muslims, is the start of God's process to create such a nation. It progresses through various stages of God *growing* the nation in Egypt; their dramatic exodus from Egypt, punishment for disobedience, wandering in the desert until the *Egyptian* generations died leaving only the younger generation, taking over the Promised Land, and establishing the nation of Israel. They now numbered in the millions, had an established system of laws and practices to worship God. God was not only instrumental in their occupation of the land, but continued to keep them safe; as long as they obeyed His laws to keep them holy. They failed miserably, and God withdrew His support as punishment in repetitive cycles until they were completely dispersed by conquering empires and finally by the Romans just after Jesus' time. This was a clear demonstration that mankind could not be holy on his own. It would require something much greater than man's ability to accomplish that.

At the flood, we reached a point in God's plan where mankind had been all but wiped out and the human race had started again through Noah's family. But that was now a long time ago and the human race had grown to millions and had settled all over the Middle East, Europe, Africa, and beyond. It was time for God to grow a people group that would eventually become His Church. He knew Abraham's heart and led him to a region that would be the homeland for the nations that would come from his seed. The land was already occupied by a number of nations, but God told Abraham that his offspring would occupy the lands of many nations currently there. This is the much abbreviated story of the creation of the nation of Israel.

God told Abram, he would have a son born to Sarai, his wife. But many years past and Sarai started to doubt God's word. She got Abram to bed her maidservant in hopes of a son and heir, as was common practice. The maid servant had a son, and called him Ishmael.

Genesis Chapter 17

¹When Abram was ninety-nine years old, the LORD appeared to him and said, "I am God Almighty; walk before me faithfully and be blameless. ²Then I will make my covenant between me and you and will greatly increase your numbers."

³Abram fell facedown, and God said to him, ⁴"As for me, this is my covenant with you: You will be the father of many nations. ⁵No longer will you be called Abram; your name will be Abraham, for I have made you a father of many nations. ⁶I will make you very fruitful; I will make nations of you, and kings will come from you. ⁷I will establish my covenant as an everlasting covenant between me and you and your descendants after you for the generations to come, to be your God and the God of your descendants after you. ⁸The whole land of Canaan, where you now reside as a foreigner, I will give as an everlasting possession to you and your descendants after you; and I will be their God."

⁹Then God said to Abraham, "As for you, you must keep my covenant, you and your descendants after you for the generations to come. ¹⁰This is my covenant with you and your descendants after you, the covenant you are to keep: Every male among you shall be circumcised. ¹¹You are to undergo circumcision, and it will be the sign of the covenant between me and you. ¹²For the generations to come every male among you who is eight days old must be circumcised, including those born in your household or bought with money from a foreigner—those who are not your offspring. ¹³Whether born in your household or bought with your money, they must be circumcised. My covenant in your flesh is to be an everlasting covenant. ¹⁴Any uncircumcised male, who has not been circumcised in the flesh, will be cut off from his people; he has broken my covenant."

¹⁵God also said to Abraham, "As for Sarai your wife, you are no longer to call her Sarai; her name will be Sarah. ¹⁶I will bless her and will surely give you a son by her. I will bless

her so that she will be the mother of nations; kings of peoples will come from her."

[17]Abraham fell facedown; he laughed and said to himself, "Will a son be born to a man a hundred years old? Will Sarah bear a child at the age of ninety?" [18]And Abraham said to God, "If only Ishmael might live under your blessing!"

[19]Then God said, "Yes, but your wife Sarah will bear you a son, and you will call him Isaac. I will establish my covenant with him as an everlasting covenant for his descendants after him. [20]And as for Ishmael, I have heard you: I will surely bless him; I will make him fruitful and will greatly increase his numbers. He will be the father of twelve rulers, and I will make him into a great nation. [21]But my covenant I will establish with Isaac, whom Sarah will bear to you by this time next year."

Abraham or rather Abram, and his wife Sarai were childless, what was worse, they were old, and Sarai was already beyond child bearing age. But what is that to the Almighty God of the universe? God renamed Abram, Abraham changing the meaning from *exalted father* to *father of many*, and Sarai, Sarah, changing its meaning from *princess* to *queen*. Of course all names have a range of meanings, but these seem most appropriate.

Genesis Chapter 18

¹The LORD appeared to Abraham near the great trees of Mamre while he was sitting at the entrance to his tent in the heat of the day. ²Abraham looked up and saw three men standing nearby. When he saw them, he hurried from the entrance of his tent to meet them and bowed low to the ground.

³He said, "If I have found favor in your eyes, my lord, do not pass your servant by. ⁴Let a little water be brought, and then you may all wash your feet and rest under this tree. ⁵Let me get you something to eat, so you can be refreshed and then go on your way—now that you have come to your servant."

"Very well," they answered, "do as you say."

⁶So Abraham hurried into the tent to Sarah. "Quick," he said, "get three seahs of the finest flour and knead it and bake some bread."

⁷Then he ran to the herd and selected a choice, tender calf and gave it to a servant, who hurried to prepare it. ⁸He then brought some curds and milk and the calf that had been prepared, and set these before them. While they ate, he stood near them under a tree.

⁹"Where is your wife Sarah?" they asked him.

"There, in the tent," he said.

¹⁰Then one of them said, "I will surely return to you about this time next year, and Sarah your wife will have a son."

Now Sarah was listening at the entrance to the tent, which was behind him. ¹¹Abraham and Sarah were already very old, and Sarah was past the age of childbearing. ¹²So Sarah laughed to herself as she thought, "After I am worn out and my lord is old, will I now have this pleasure?"

¹³Then the LORD said to Abraham, "Why did Sarah laugh and say, 'Will I really have a child, now that I am old?' ¹⁴Is anything too hard for the LORD? I will return to you at the appointed time next year, and Sarah will have a son."

¹⁵Sarah was afraid, so she lied and said, "I did not laugh."

But he said, "Yes, you did laugh."

God had big plans for Abraham's family, starting with his son Isaac, but he did not discount Ishmael, a son born years earlier by his wife's handmaid. Ishmael was likely the father of many of the Arab nations of today, probably intermixed with some of the nations that existed in the region in Abraham's time. You would have expected God to give Abraham many sons to get the family line off to a good start, but it wasn't time for the family to explode. Regardless of how Abraham was supposed to take over the whole of Canaan, it was already occupied by a number of squabbling, but established nations and city states. Even if his family grew to hundreds and maybe even thousands, he would be just one of many antagonistic clans. It would be an uphill struggle, even with God's help to overcome his rivals; his clan would just lack the numbers to *occupy* a vast region.

Isaac

It would take two more generations for God to start expanding the family. Probably with God's promise in mind, Abraham acquired a wife for His son Isaac from his own country, and his own people. God's hand was obviously in this remarkable mission to find a wife for his son; the story is well worth a read in Genesis Chapter 24. Isaac had two sons, Jacob and Esau, who were as different as chalk and cheese.

Jacob

Jacob, somewhat of a scoundrel, was born grasping Esau's ankle, and he was appropriately named Jacob, meaning *holder of the heel* or maybe more colloquially *grabber*, *usurper*, or *supplanter*. He conned Esau out of his birthright, where he would get a double portion of the inheritance from Isaac, and later tricked his half blind father into giving him Esau's, the first born's blessing. Jacob was more of a *home boy*, whereas Esau was a hunting man, rugged and capable.

Genesis Chapter 27

[19] *Jacob said to his father, "I am Esau your firstborn. I have done as you told me. Please sit up and eat some of my game, so that you may give me your blessing."*

[20] *Isaac asked his son, "How did you find it so quickly, my son?"*

"The LORD your God gave me success," he replied.

²¹Then Isaac said to Jacob, *"Come near so I can touch you, my son, to know whether you really are my son Esau or not."*

²²Jacob went close to his father Isaac, who touched him and said, *"The voice is the voice of Jacob, but the hands are the hands of Esau."* ²³He did not recognize him, for his hands were hairy like those of his brother Esau; so he proceeded to bless him. ²⁴*"Are you really my son Esau?"* he asked.

"I am," he replied.

²⁵Then he said, *"My son, bring me some of your game to eat, so that I may give you my blessing."*

Jacob brought it to him and he ate; and he brought some wine and he drank. ²⁶Then his father Isaac said to him, *"Come here, my son, and kiss me."*

²⁷So he went to him and kissed him. When Isaac caught the smell of his clothes, he blessed him and said, *"Ah, the smell of my son is like the smell of a field that the LORD has blessed.* ²⁸*May God give you heaven's dew and earth's richness—an abundance of grain and new wine.* ²⁹*May nations serve you and peoples bow down to you. Be lord over your brothers, and may the sons of your mother bow down to you. May those who curse you be cursed and those who bless you be blessed."*

³⁰After Isaac finished blessing him, and Jacob had scarcely left his father's presence, his brother Esau came in from

hunting. ³¹*He too prepared some tasty food and brought it to his father. Then he said to him, "My father, please sit up and eat some of my game, so that you may give me your blessing."*

³²*His father Isaac asked him, "Who are you?"*

"I am your son," he answered, "your firstborn, Esau."

³³*Isaac trembled violently and said, "Who was it, then, that hunted game and brought it to me? I ate it just before you came and I blessed him—and indeed he will be blessed!"*

³⁴*When Esau heard his father's words, he burst out with a loud and bitter cry and said to his father, "Bless me—me too, my father!"*

³⁵*But he said, "Your brother came deceitfully and took your blessing."*

³⁶*Esau said, "Isn't he rightly named Jacob? This is the second time he has taken advantage of me: He took my birthright, and now he's taken my blessing!" Then he asked, "Haven't you reserved any blessing for me?"*

³⁷*Isaac answered Esau, "I have made him lord over you and have made all his relatives his servants, and I have sustained him with grain and new wine. So what can I possibly do for you, my son?"*

³⁸*Esau said to his father, "Do you have only one blessing, my father? Bless me too, my father!" Then Esau wept aloud.*

³⁹His father Isaac answered him, "Your dwelling will be away from the earth's richness, away from the dew of heaven above. ⁴⁰You will live by the sword and you will serve your brother. But when you grow restless, you will throw his yoke from off your neck."

⁴¹Esau held a grudge against Jacob because of the blessing his father had given him. He said to himself, "The days of mourning for my father are near; then I will kill my brother Jacob."

Jacob's con tricks caused Esau to voice threats against Jacob's very life, so at his mother's suggestion, Jacob wisely went off to live with an uncle, Laban, the brother of his father's wife Rebekah. Maybe as a lesson, or was it just God's humour that placed Jacob under the crafty Laban's thumb for 20 years, while he paid Laban for his daughter Rachel, but not before Laban tricked him into marrying Leah, his older and less appealing daughter. Laban seemed almost more cunning than Jacob, substituting Leah for Rachel on Rachel's wedding night. Now married to Leah, but still not Rachel, Jacob had to agree to another seven years for Rachel. Jacob agreed to work seven years for each of Laban's daughters, but ended up staying another six years in the less than cordial relationship with Laban to grow his own flocks. Sometimes it seems that God wants the books to balance before He uses someone. Maybe God balanced Jacob's dealings with Esau with Jacob's treatment by Laban; regardless, it definitely seems a case of what goes around comes around.

God had continued the same covenant with Isaac that He had made with Abraham and now God was establishing a relationship with Jacob. He started by giving Jacob a vision while he was on his way to Laban. By the time Jacob decided to sneak away from Laban and return to Canaan, he had twelve sons; the sons who became the nations of Israel. God has bigger plans than us and despite Jacob's love for Rachel eclipsing his love, if any, for Leah, Leah bore Jacob his first four sons, including Judah, the family line of Jesus. Later Leah had two more sons after, Rachel had her first. In her desperation Rachel gave her servants to Jacob, to bear sons for her, as that was a common practice. The servants bore Jacob four sons between them, but finally Rachel, his favourite, gave Jacob his two youngest sons, first Joseph, and then Benjamin. God had blessed Abraham and Isaac in strange ways so that they were both very rich, but Jacob was a self-made man, even if by very circuitous way – you'll just have to read the story in Genesis Chapter 30. How often the sayings in Proverbs come true; Jacob had a plan to take Rachel for his wife, but God guided his steps, and married him to Leah as well, to get the nation of Israel off to a good start as far as sons go. Rachel in the end only gave Jacob two sons; God's plan was for twelve sons.

A great deal of bitterness had developed between Jacob and Laban's sons, and also Rachel and Leah against their father Laban.

Genesis Chapter 31

³Then the LORD said to Jacob, "Go back to the land of your fathers and to your relatives, and I will be with you."

With this prompting, Joseph found an opportunity to escape the whole situation and took it. Secretly he made a run back to Canaan, to the land of his father Isaac. Laban's family apparently did not have a relationship with God and had family idols, probably made of gold. When they left, Rachel stole the idols, justifying it in her mind by agreeing with Leah, that they would not inherit anything from their father.

Was it Satan trying to put a spoke in the works by enticing Rachel to steal her father Laban's family idols? After three days Laban caught up with Jacob, his flocks, servants, goods, and wives, angry that Jacob had snuck off, and stolen his valuable idols to boot. Jacob innocently offered a search, which Laban did, but Rachel, feigning her period, hid them in the saddle she sat on. Eventually, having settled affairs with Laban amicably, Joseph set off for Canaan, but soon met up with some angels.

Genesis Chapter 32

¹Jacob also went on his way, and the angels of God met him. ² When Jacob saw them, he said, "This is the camp of God!" So he named that place Mahanaim.

This is a very brief statement of encounter, and reveals nothing about what was said. Possibly he was warned that

Esau would meet him, and more importantly it was likely that it was preparation of the upcoming show down with God himself. Jacob had maintained his relationship with the God of his father Isaac, and grandfather Abraham. Isaac must have instructed his sons in the ways of God, circumcising them as instructed in the Abraham's covenant with God. But the true relationship must have started when he was fleeing Esau on his way to Laban, when he had a dream of angels descending and ascending a ladder from heaven. It was obviously a very significant dream as Joseph set up an altar the next morning, pouring a drink offering out on it.

Free of Laban, Jacob carried on but prepared a lavish gift of livestock to placate his brother. Esau, hearing that Jacob was coming, went out to meet him with a large number of men, obviously enjoying making Jacob fear for his life, in the mock confrontation. I think that may have been the final part of the penalty set by God to satisfy His justice, and setting a large slice of very humble pie before Jacob. It also served to clean the slate between the brothers so Jacob could start afresh in peace. His servants went ahead with the livestock and met up with Esau and his four hundred men, but Esau continued on to meet Jacob. The servants returned to Joseph with the news. Jacob was truly rattled, and was heading right into a confrontation, more perceived than real, with his brother Esau. Jacob seriously feared for the lives of his family. Fortunately God had blessed Esau, and his need for revenge had been sated by having a large family and large flocks of his own.

The real major event however on this journey of escape from Laban was not in the upcoming meeting with his brother, but was with his encounter with God. The previous night, as Jacob and his clan neared Esau, Jacob split his clan into two groups, hoping to salvage one half, if the reunion with Esau turned out for the worse. Jacob slept alone that night and was awake all night *wrestling* with a man, who he came to understand was God himself. This has to be one of the strangest encounters with the Almighty every recorded in the Bible. It seems that God, most likely Jesus, was actually manifested as a man, as besides wrestling there was conversation.

Genesis Chapter 32

[22]That night Jacob got up and took his two wives, his two female servants and his eleven sons and crossed the ford of the Jabbok. [23]After he had sent them across the stream, he sent over all his possessions. [24]So Jacob was left alone, and a man wrestled with him till daybreak. [25]When the man saw that he could not overpower him, he touched the socket of Jacob's hip so that his hip was wrenched as he wrestled with the man. [26]Then the man said, "Let me go, for it is daybreak."

But Jacob replied, "I will not let you go unless you bless me."

[27]The man asked him, "What is your name?"

"Jacob," he answered.

²⁸Then the man said, "Your name will no longer be Jacob, but Israel, because you have struggled with God and with humans and have overcome."

²⁹Jacob said, "Please tell me your name."

But he replied, "Why do you ask my name?" Then he blessed him there.

³⁰So Jacob called the place Peniel, saying, "It is because I saw God face to face, and yet my life was spared."

³¹The sun rose above him as he passed Peniel, and he was limping because of his hip. ³²Therefore to this day the Israelites do not eat the tendon attached to the socket of the hip, because the socket of Jacob's hip was touched near the tendon.

This was possibly a metaphor for Jacob's spiritual struggle and submission to God. Jacob must have mellowed somewhat, compared to his scheming youth, but that streak was still strong as described in Genesis, during the last six years with Laban while he built up his flocks. Jacob had some bizarre ideas about how to breed the flocks to his advantage. I think God would have blessed him anyway, and maybe this was Jacob trying to do it in his own strength. He must have spent a lot of energy scheming, and his time with Laban, who was constantly trying to cheat Jacob, must have been a wearing time.

There were probably many interactions between God and Jacob since he left his parents, and this encounter with God may have in some way been the equivalent of Abraham's testing by God when He asked Abraham to sacrifice Isaac. This encounter with God was a landmark event, but instead of the common mound of stones used to mark significant events, God gave Joseph a living monument, maybe so he would remember the event clearly for the rest of his life. After finally meeting up with Esau, Jacob wisely decided to put some distance between himself and Esau by heading back in another direction to find a good place to settle.

These Chapters in Genesis describe the sculpting of Jacob, while the next significant step in God's plan to build a nation switched to Joseph, Rachel's son. Jacob had a rough ride with his uncle Laban, but he left with huge flocks and 12 sons, the eventual tribes of Israel. God had renamed Jacob, Israel, and his 12 sons who were to form the basis of the nation were off to a rocky start. Jacob was somewhat obtuse. He conned his brother Esau out of his birthright with a bowl of stew, and because his father Isaac was almost blind, and at the bidding of his mother, he even stole Isaac's blessing on the first born by impersonating Esau. For the many years he lived with Laban, he did not reap a blessing, but one load of work, while God balanced the books. But God brings good from bad, and it was there where the 12 tribes of Israel were birthed. What was Jacob thinking; how could he have possibly got away with his outrageous cons? Now as the patriarch of his own family, he was just as obtuse as he was in his youth. But now, away from Laban, and having made peace with Esau things were going better, with most of the credit probably due to God. God had arranged for Jacob to escape the anger of Esau, who had threatened Jacobs's life, and to have a large number of sons. He returned from his uncle Laban a wealthy man, with flocks and servants.

Joseph

Joseph was Jacob's first son by the love of his life, Rachel. He probably spoiled Joseph openly, much to the irritation of his brothers. Joseph seems to have inherited the obtuse genes and even though his dreams foretelling the future were from God, instead of keeping the self-aggrandising dreams to himself he tells his family that "they will bow down to him." Despite the fact that these dreams were to come true, and it was God foretelling the future, God had stacked the deck with Jacob's and Joseph's genes so that Joseph's days would be numbered one way or another. The final straw came with the innocent *coat of many colours* that Jacob thoughtlessly gave to Joseph, as an obvious display of favouritism. Then Joseph proceeded to parade before his brothers.

Judah, the eldest brother cracked. Joseph, nearly killed, lived another day, but now as a slave, sold to a passing caravan of traders headed for Egypt. Things were not off to a good start, but what would seem to be an insurmountable challenge for a man was actually part of God's plan. It seems that God guides and pats His plans along so that *things just happen as things normally would*.

Jacob was now living as an alien in the land of Canaan, the land was occupied, and as his family expanded, it would threaten the indigenous peoples. It is unlikely that he would have had a successful time creating a great nation without ongoing number- reducing conflicts with the locals. But not just the locals; God had promised a vast area to Abraham, from the Sinai, to the Euphrates to the Mediterranean. The whole land was occupied. How do you procreate such a large number of people, from Jacob's family of some tens, so that they could occupy such a vast area in safety? God's plan had started with Abraham, who proved himself worthy to be the father of God's nation. He instructed Isaac in God's ways. Isaac in turn passed the ways of God onto his sons Jacob and Esau, and Jacob onto his 12 sons, but it seems Joseph was blessed with Jacob's obtuse genes. They must have made a right pair; but it set the circumstances, which triggered a series of events that you couldn't make up.

Joseph goes off to Egypt, and gets sold to one of the pharaohs' officials. God blesses him, while I'm sure letting him learn a lesson in humility. It doesn't take long for God to end humility 101, and enrol Joseph in humility 201. The official's wife takes a fancy to Joseph, and is herself enraged and humiliated by Joseph's rejection of her, even though it was out of loyalty to his master, and faithfulness to God. The wife trumps up attempted rape charges and Joseph is carted off to prison, where the course humility 201 is about to start. God is gentle, knowing that Joseph is but a pawn in His plan, and blesses Joseph during his stay in the prison. He is put in charge by the head jailer. While he's there he encounters two other inmates who have dreams. God interprets the dreams for Joseph who correctly relates the reality to them, in which one will live while the other will die upon their release. It takes a couple of years, but then this crucial step in God's plan of interpreting dreams kicks into gear. God has arranged that His weather for the next 14 years would dominate events of the entire region of Egypt, Canaan, and beyond.

Pharaoh has two troubling dreams and is so troubled by them that he calls all his magicians to interpret them for him, but they cannot. At this point, Pharaoh's cupbearer, who'd had his dream interpreted in prison by Joseph years earlier, and who was released and lived, recounts this event to Pharaoh. Joseph is summoned, and acknowledging God for the interpretation, eloquently interprets Pharaoh's dreams.

Genesis Chapter 41

[1] When two full years had passed, Pharaoh had a dream: He was standing by the Nile, [2] when out of the river there came up seven cows, sleek and fat, and they grazed among the reeds. [3] After them, seven other cows, ugly and gaunt, came up out of the Nile and stood beside those on the riverbank. [4] And the cows that were ugly and gaunt ate up the seven sleek, fat cows. Then Pharaoh woke up.

[5] He fell asleep again and had a second dream: Seven heads of grain, healthy and good, were growing on a single stalk. [6] After them, seven other heads of grain sprouted—thin and scorched by the east wind. [7] The thin heads of grain

swallowed up the seven healthy, full heads. Then Pharaoh woke up; it had been a dream.

Then Pharaoh woke up; it had been a dream. The interpretation is summed up in a few verses.

Genesis Chapter 41

[28]"It is just as I said to Pharaoh: God has shown Pharaoh what he is about to do. [29]Seven years of great abundance are coming throughout the land of Egypt, [30]but seven years of famine will follow them. Then all the abundance in Egypt will be forgotten, and the famine will ravage the land.

This was a grand claim, but Pharaoh, possibly with God's assistance bought into it. If it were true, Joseph had just saved his nation from calamity, even bringing it to the brink of annihilation, to say nothing of the surrounding region. For now Pharaoh was so grateful to Joseph that he makes him only second to himself, so that he can carry out his plan to store the grain in the years of plenty to provide for the lean years. I'm sure Pharaoh's attitude would have changed if Joseph's interpretation had not panned out; but this was God's plan, there's no way it could not pan out.

Now for the really cool part; after the seven years of plenty, the first year of famine arrived. Jacob's family like many of the others in the region was affected. The grain crops failed. They had preserves, such as dried dates and figs, but no grain, for bread. Like many others in Canaan, Jacob had heard that there was grain in Egypt. He sent some of his sons with payment to buy grain from Egypt. Presumably at God's urging, Joseph who after at least ten years looks like an Egyptian, having heard that there were Hebrews asking to buy grain, serves his brothers personally. For some reason he invokes an elaborate scheme; he accuses them of spying and keeps one of them as hostage as penalty. His dream had come true on his brothers' first visit to buy grain; they bowed down to him!

Genesis Chapter 42

6Now Joseph was the governor of the land, the one who sold grain to all his people. So when Joseph's brothers arrived, they bowed down to him with their faces to the ground.

It is strange that Joseph, now in the midst of his immense survival strategy, has the time to keep tabs on which foreigners are coming to buy grain; was Joseph aware of God's plan, had he linked his own dreams and God's unfolding plan? Regardless, the ruse plays out and Jacob is forced to send more sons to get more grain and the saga continues. Eventually, Joseph gets his brothers to return to Egypt with Benjamin, his brother, the son of Joseph's mother, Rachel.

Genesis Chapter 43

29As he looked about and saw his brother Benjamin, his own mother's son, he asked, "Is this your youngest brother, the one you told me about?" And he said, "God be gracious to you, my son." 30Deeply moved at the sight of his brother,

Joseph hurried out and looked for a place to weep. He went into his private room and wept there. ³¹After he had washed his face, he came out and, controlling himself, said, "Serve the food." ³²They served him by himself, the brothers by themselves, and the Egyptians who ate with him by themselves, because Egyptians could not eat with Hebrews, for that is detestable to Egyptians. ³³The men had been seated before him in the order of their ages, from the firstborn to the youngest; and they looked at each other in astonishment. ³⁴When portions were served to them from Joseph's table, Benjamin's portion was five times as much as anyone else's. So they feasted and drank freely with him.

Joseph sends them on their way with their silver and his *divination* cup in their sacks, but he sends his servant after them to accuse them and find it; they return to Joseph. Joseph can keep up the pretense no longer and reveals himself to his brothers, who are literally scared to death that Joseph is going to wreak retribution on them for selling him as a slave. It is a very emotional reunion, as Joseph explains that this was God's plan all along, and for them not to blame themselves.

Genesis Chapter 45

¹Then Joseph could no longer control himself before all his attendants and he cried out, "Have everyone leave my presence!" So there was no one with Joseph when he made himself known to his brothers. ²And he wept so loudly that the

Egyptians heard him, and Pharaoh's household heard about it.

³Joseph said to his brothers, "I am Joseph! Is my father still living?" But his brothers were not able to answer him, because they were terrified at his presence.

⁴Then Joseph said to his brothers, "Come close to me." When they had done so, he said, "I am your brother Joseph, the one you sold into Egypt! ⁵And now, do not be distressed and do not be angry with yourselves for selling me here, because it was to save lives that God sent me ahead of you. ⁶For two years now there has been famine in the land, and for the next five years there will be no plowing and reaping. ⁷But God sent me ahead of you to preserve for you a remnant on earth and to save your lives by a great deliverance.

⁸"So then, it was not you who sent me here, but God. He made me father to Pharaoh, lord of his entire household and ruler of all Egypt. ⁹Now hurry back to my father and say to him, 'This is what your son Joseph says: God has made me lord of all Egypt. Come down to me; don't delay. ¹⁰You shall live in the region of Goshen and be near me—you, your children and grandchildren, your flocks and herds, and all you have. ¹¹I will provide for you there, because five years of famine are still to come. Otherwise you and your household and all who belong to you will become destitute.'

It's almost as if Joseph is having a little retribution fun as he seats them in order of age, but I don't think so, it seems like he was bursting to tell them his real identity all along. Maybe

God outlined this plan in a dream to get his family to move; if he had just revealed himself at the outset, maybe they would have been so scared of retribution they would never have returned. God always seems to have subplots in play, and this was probably one of them. Joseph's subterfuge with his brothers seems either another case of God's justice, or God's discipline. In the lived out reality this may be just semantics depending on whether you are one of God's children, but as they became the tribes of Israel I think it was a combination of discipline and a demonstration of His power.

Joseph tells his brothers to return to their father and to bring all his family, flocks, and herds to Egypt. God speaks to Jacob, Israel, reassuring him about going to Egypt and they all come, and with the blessing of the Pharaoh they are settled in Goshen, a most fertile area by the Nile. Jacob's household, is now well taken care of for the seven year's famine, and is able to grow as fast as any people group could on the face of the earth, particularly with God's blessing.

If they were still in Canaan they would have problem but they are safe; they are under the protection of Pharaoh of Egypt, ruler of the most powerful nation on earth at that time. This goes on for 430 years, and the Israelite population grows to over 2 million! Unfortunately after a few centuries, the courts of the Pharaoh forget that Joseph was their saviour during the famine, when God revealed what was going to happen in the region. Egypt, along with the whole region would have been decimated. As it was, by the end of the famine Pharaoh, who owned all the stored grain, had sold it to his subjects in exchange for their money, livestock and land. It was a very severe time, but all the while the nation of Israel was booming. Fear of the populous Israelites grew and various laws were passed to curb their growth. Long before the end of the 430 years they were enslaved, but their numbers still grew.

Of all the places on earth Egypt was the probably the best place to grow a nation rapidly. If they had stayed in Canaan just buying grain, they would have been as destitute as the Egyptian populous. If they had tried to migrate on their own to Egypt they would have been second class citizens and destitute. What a miraculous plan to have Joseph go there ahead of the famine and become as influential as you can get, all by tweaking the character of Jacob and Joseph. Joseph had obviously developed a deep relationship with God as when his family was reunited he repeatedly told his brothers that it had been God's will all along. Nevertheless Joseph's brothers were still afraid that Joseph might seek revenge when their father, Jacob, died and his protective influence was lost.

Genesis Chapter 50

[19] But Joseph said to them, "Don't be afraid. Am I in the place of God? [20] You intended to harm me, but God intended it for good to accomplish what is now being done, the saving of many lives. [21] So then, don't be afraid. I will provide for you and your children." And he reassured them and spoke kindly to them.

Moses

The Egyptians became afraid of the numbers of Hebrews (Israelites) in Egypt, and Pharaoh ordered that all their male babies be thrown into the Nile to limit the Hebrew population growth. Moses a Hebrew was miraculously rescued and raised by Pharaoh's daughter after being set adrift in the reeds of the Nile banks. When Moses was about 40 years old he sensed God's calling on his life. He was raised in Pharaoh's court as a prince, but triggered his own exile by doing it his way. Moses murdered an Egyptian who was mistreating a Hebrew slave, and when this became public knowledge he ran away to Midian, where he married and lived as a sheepherder for forty years. I suspect this was God's plan B, as the Israelites were in Egypt for a little over the 400 years predicted in the Bible. Moses' impulsive behaviour was moderated by talking to sheep for forty years; everything slows down around sheep. His rash exterior was worn down by sheer time and smoothed like a stone in a polishing drum. This was not an uncommon event for God to take those who He would use mightily, through a time of refinement, to renew their minds, to become more like Jesus. Almost the opposite in nature now 40 years later, Moses tries to wriggle out of the role that God tries to lay on him at the burning bush. Finally Moses very reluctantly agrees to return to Egypt, confront the new Pharaoh, with his brother Aaron as his mouthpiece, to demand that he release the Israelites from captivity and let them leave Egypt.

Now one of my dots is right here in these passages, and I think it is mentioned more than once. God *hardens* pharaoh's heart. It seems God just uses certain people for His purposes sometimes. I'm sure that God already *knew* that these people would never bend the knee to Him, and so were fair game. Even when people like Nebuchadnezzar acknowledged God, they did not follow Him. It will be interesting to see if they make it to heaven. Even Pharaoh, when he finally relents, believing in the power of the God of the Hebrews, asks Moses to bless him. People in that time believed that each nation had its own gods, so you could believe in someone else's god without taking that god to be your own god. Maybe they didn't even believe they could. Regardless it would have been politically catastrophic for any ruler to do that. Akhenaten, Tutankhamun's father, who tried to replace the polytheistic Egyptian gods with the single god Aten, failed as the priests, probably coercing Tutankhamun, reverted to their original gods, when he died.

Moses heads off to Egypt armed with a host of miracles to perform, all seemingly to demonstrate the impotency of the host of fabricated Egyptian deities. Read the whole deployment of these miracles, and the *ok go* and *no I've changed my mind* responses from Pharaoh that lace through the saga in Exodus Chapter 8. God not only wanted to demonstrate His power to the Egyptians but also the Israelites, who, I'm sure, had been losing their faith in God since they had been in slavery.

The miracles, although extremely impressive and only initially matched by the Pharaoh's magicians, seem to fade very quickly in the minds of the Hebrew population. Interestingly it is obviously not the magicians who had the power, but demons, acting out their magic; this was a proxy war by God and Satan! God has set limits on what He allows Satan and the demons to do. This is true, for men also, as Jesus confers power on 70 of His disciples, temporarily allowing them to heal and cast out demons. Eventually the last miracle for the Hebrews, or plague for the Egyptians, the killing of the first born of men and livestock, was the clincher. It is still honoured today as the Feast of the Unleavened Bread, when the Spirit of God *passed over* the Israelite children because they daubed blood of the Passover Lamb on their door posts.

Exodus Chapter 12

²⁹At midnight the LORD *struck down all the firstborn in Egypt, from the firstborn of Pharaoh, who sat on the throne, to the firstborn of the prisoner, who was in the dungeon, and the firstborn of all the livestock as well. ³⁰Pharaoh and all his officials and all the Egyptians got up during the night, and there was loud wailing in Egypt, for there was not a house without someone dead.*

³¹During the night Pharaoh summoned Moses and Aaron and said, "Up! Leave my people, you and the Israelites! Go, worship the LORD *as you have requested. ³²Take your flocks and herds, as you have said, and go. And also bless me."*

> ³³The Egyptians urged the people to hurry and leave the country, "For otherwise," they said, "we will all die!" ³⁴So the people took their dough before the yeast was added, and carried it on their shoulders in kneading troughs wrapped in clothing. ³⁵The Israelites did as Moses instructed and asked the Egyptians for articles of silver and gold and for clothing. ³⁶The LORD had made the Egyptians favorably disposed toward the people, and they gave them what they asked for; so they plundered the Egyptians.

Pharaoh relented, Moses told the Israelites to ask their Egyptian neighbours for expensive cloth, jewels, and articles of precious metals. When they left Egypt, they numbered over 600,000 men of fighting age, plus all the women and children; they took all their flocks and all the booty that the Egyptians were only too ready to give them if they would only leave Egypt.

The Exodus

The Israelites move out early, heading out across the desert until they hit the Red Sea, where, a week after an amazingly selective miracle that kills only the Egyptian firstborn children and livestock, they start to whine. The whine that sky is falling on their head and they will die at the hand of the Egyptians in the desert. Admittedly the Red Sea was in front of them, and Pharaoh, who had been persuaded by his officials to go after them, and all his chariots and army followed the Israelites and were now just on the other side of God's pillar of cloud. God had given the Israelites a pillar of cloud that guided them during the day which turned to a pillar of fire at night, so they did not have to stop at night. They must have rested though as it had been seven days since they left Egypt. This would be the first of a series of whining episodes by the Israelites about being brought out of Egypt only to die, despite God having demonstrated His power so explicitly in their favour. True they must have been physically and mentally exhausted, and even though they had seen great miracles they were not miracles of protection, although they had not suffered from any of the plagues on Egypt.

On the other side of the pillar of cloud and fire, cloud on the Egyptian side and fire on the Israelite side, Pharaoh was in the dark, but the Israelites had light during the night. They could hear the horses, hundreds, maybe thousands of them and their unmistakable odour, they could hear men's shouts and the clanging of their weapons. They were scared out of their wits, the cloud was all that stood between them and certain death. Pharaoh's army had lost many men in the last plague of the first born, as many of their comrades, some even brothers, would have been first born and inexplicably died overnight.

It was only a week ago and they knew it was by the hand of the Israelite's God, and the frustrated men of the Egyptian army wanted revenge; they could taste it, their prey was only a hundred feet away. The living mass of a few million were now in a panic, they had been funnelled by a canyon to a beach on the Red Sea. They were hemmed in by the canyon walls, the enraged mighty Egyptian army just the other side of the pillar of cloud and fire, and the Sea. They felt near to death, hopeless. Desperately they pleaded with Moses "call on your God to save us." The miracles of God were too recent; they had no trust in a God who had shown up all of a sudden, even with spectacular miracles. God had got them released, but only to land them in a more precarious predicament than they were in Egypt at the mercy of the Egyptians. In general humans do not like surprises or changes, especially bad ones. Traipsing through the desert for days, now they were close to death and were dependent on a God they could only *see* in the impersonal Pillar of Cloud and Pillar of Fire. Sure, He could turn water to blood and bring plagues of frogs, but how could that help them?

In another amazing miracle, God parts the Red Sea, not only to allow the fleeing Israelites passage, but also in a spectacular twist, to wipe out Pharaoh's army without a battle, or even one Israelite raising a sword.

Exodus Chapter 14

[15]Then the LORD said to Moses, "Why are you crying out to me? Tell the Israelites to move on. [16]Raise your staff and stretch out your hand over the sea to divide the water so that the Israelites can go through the sea on dry ground. [17]I will harden the hearts of the Egyptians so that they will go in after them. And I will gain glory through Pharaoh and all his army, through his chariots and his horsemen. [18]The

Egyptians will know that I am the LORD when I gain glory through Pharaoh, his chariots and his horsemen."

[19] Then the angel of God, who had been traveling in front of Israel's army, withdrew and went behind them. The pillar of cloud also moved from in front and stood behind them, [20] coming between the armies of Egypt and Israel. Throughout the night the cloud brought darkness to the one side and light to the other side; so neither went near the other all night long.

[21] Then Moses stretched out his hand over the sea, and all that night the LORD drove the sea back with a strong east wind and turned it into dry land. The waters were divided, [22] and the Israelites went through the sea on dry ground, with a wall of water on their right and on their left.

[23] The Egyptians pursued them, and all Pharaoh's horses and chariots and horsemen followed them into the sea. [24] During the last watch of the night the LORD looked down from the pillar of fire and cloud at the Egyptian army and threw it into confusion. [25] He jammed the wheels of their chariots so that they had difficulty driving. And the Egyptians said, "Let's get away from the Israelites! The LORD is fighting for them against Egypt."

[26] Then the LORD said to Moses, "Stretch out your hand over the sea so that the waters may flow back over the Egyptians and their chariots and horsemen." [27] Moses stretched out his hand over the sea, and at daybreak the sea went back to its place. The Egyptians were fleeing toward it, and the LORD

swept them into the sea. *²⁸The water flowed back and covered the chariots and horsemen—the entire army of Pharaoh that had followed the Israelites into the sea. Not one of them survived.*

²⁹But the Israelites went through the sea on dry ground, with a wall of water on their right and on their left. ³⁰That day the LORD saved Israel from the hands of the Egyptians, and Israel saw the Egyptians lying dead on the shore.

After having devastated the land itself with the 10 plagues that God, through Moses, brought on Egypt ruining it economically, Pharaoh's army now disappears under the waters of the Red Sea. This effectively gets Pharaoh off their case forever. This event was so dramatic that it went ahead of them and into the Promised Land and was still associated with the Israelites over 40 years later. What a spectacular event to witness. God, above the previous plagues, demonstrates His complete dominance over a nation coming against His nation, Israel; glorifying Himself, and you would think, convincing the people that He is their invincible guardian. Would that be an end to their skepticism? No, only days later they are bleating about water. At an oasis God turns bitter water to sweet, and then they complain about not having meat. Fortunately God has a lot more patience than me, but even that has its limits.

Exodus Chapter 16

⁶So Moses and Aaron said to all the Israelites, "In the evening you will know that it was the LORD who brought you out of Egypt, ^{7}and in the morning you will see the glory of the LORD, because he has heard your grumbling against him. Who are we, that you should grumble against us?" ^{8}Moses also said, "You will know that it was the LORD when he gives you meat to eat in the evening and all the bread you want in the morning, because he has heard your grumbling against him. Who are we? You are not grumbling against us, but against the LORD."

^{9}Then Moses told Aaron, "Say to the entire Israelite community, 'Come before the LORD, for he has heard your grumbling'."

^{10} While Aaron was speaking to the whole Israelite community, they looked toward the desert, and there was the glory of the LORD appearing in the cloud.

^{11}The LORD said to Moses, ^{12}"I have heard the grumbling of the Israelites. Tell them, 'At twilight you will eat meat, and in the morning you will be filled with bread. Then you will know that I am the LORD your God'."

^{13}That evening quail came and covered the camp, and in the morning there was a layer of dew around the camp. ^{14}When the dew was gone, thin flakes like frost on the ground appeared on the desert floor.

I think God must be English because another time they were whining about not having meat it seems His sarcasm comes out while providing the meat. It is clear God is getting really angry at His whining nation.

Numbers Chapter 11

³¹Now a wind went out from the LORD and drove quail in from the sea. It scattered them up to two cubits deep all around the camp, as far as a day's walk in any direction. ³²All that day and night and all the next day the people went out and gathered quail. No one gathered less than ten homers. Then they spread them out all around the camp. ³³But while the meat was still between their teeth and before it could be consumed, the anger of the LORD burned against the people, and he struck them with a severe plague. ³⁴Therefore the place was named Kibroth Hattaavah, because there they buried the people who had craved other food.

Two cubits is about 3 ft or almost 1m, the amount was a few tons in total. His anger was evident as many died when they ate this meat.

This goes on and on, until they reach the borders of the Promised Land, the vast lands God promised to Abraham. God has made His covenant with His people by now. They have the Ten Commandments inscribed by the finger of God on stone tablets, the second set; Moses had smashed the first set when he returned from the mountain and found the Israelites worshiping a golden calf! What would you do if you were God? God wanted to kill them all, but Moses pleaded to God to let them live. However God is constrained by His justice. It had to be satisfied, and it was.

Exodus Chapter 32

¹When the people saw that Moses was so long in coming down from the mountain, they gathered around Aaron and said, "Come, make us gods who will go before us. As for this fellow Moses who brought us up out of Egypt, we don't know what has happened to him."

²Aaron answered them, "Take off the gold earrings that your wives, your sons and your daughters are wearing, and bring them to me." ³So all the people took off their earrings and brought them to Aaron. ⁴He took what they handed him and made it into an idol cast in the shape of a calf, fashioning it with a tool. Then they said, "These are your gods, Israel, who brought you up out of Egypt."

⁵When Aaron saw this, he built an altar in front of the calf and announced, "Tomorrow there will be a festival to the LORD." ⁶So the next day the people rose early and sacrificed burnt offerings and presented fellowship offerings. Afterward they sat down to eat and drink and got up to indulge in revelry.

⁷Then the LORD said to Moses, "Go down, because your people, whom you brought up out of Egypt, have become corrupt. ⁸They have been quick to turn away from what I commanded them and have made themselves an idol cast in the shape of a calf. They have bowed down to it and sacrificed to it and have said, 'These are your gods, Israel, who brought you up out of Egypt.'

⁹"I have seen these people," the LORD said to Moses, "and they are a stiff-necked people. ¹⁰Now leave me alone so that my anger may burn against them and that I may destroy them. Then I will make you into a great nation."

¹¹But Moses sought the favor of the LORD his God. "LORD," he said, "why should your anger burn against your people, whom you brought out of Egypt with great power and a mighty hand? ¹²Why should the Egyptians say, 'It was with evil intent that he brought them out, to kill them in the mountains and to wipe them off the face of the earth'? Turn from your fierce anger; relent and do not bring disaster on your people. ¹³Remember your servants Abraham, Isaac and Israel, to whom you swore by your own self: 'I will make your descendants as numerous as the stars in the sky and I will give your descendants all this land I promised them, and it will be their inheritance forever'." ¹⁴Then the LORD relented and did not bring on his people the disaster he had threatened.

¹⁵Moses turned and went down the mountain with the two tablets of the covenant law in his hands. They were inscribed on both sides, front and back. ¹⁶The tablets were the work of God; the writing was the writing of God, engraved on the tablets.

¹⁷When Joshua heard the noise of the people shouting, he said to Moses, "There is the sound of war in the camp."

¹⁸Moses replied: "It is not the sound of victory, it is not the sound of defeat; it is the sound of singing that I hear."

¹⁹*When Moses approached the camp and saw the calf and the dancing, his anger burned and he threw the tablets out of his hands, breaking them to pieces at the foot of the mountain. ²⁰And he took the calf the people had made and burned it in the fire; then he ground it to powder, scattered it on the water and made the Israelites drink it.*

²¹*He said to Aaron, "What did these people do to you, that you led them into such great sin?"*

²²*"Do not be angry, my lord," Aaron answered. "You know how prone these people are to evil. ²³They said to me, 'Make us gods who will go before us. As for this fellow Moses who brought us up out of Egypt, we don't know what has happened to him.' ²⁴So I told them, 'Whoever has any gold jewelry, take it off.' Then they gave me the gold, and I threw it into the fire, and out came this calf!"*

²⁵*Moses saw that the people were running wild and that Aaron had let them get out of control and so become a laughingstock to their enemies. ²⁶So he stood at the entrance to the camp and said, "Whoever is for the* LORD, *come to me." And all the Levites rallied to him.*

²⁷*Then he said to them, "This is what the* LORD, *the God of Israel, says: 'Each man strap a sword to his side. Go back and forth through the camp from one end to the other, each killing his brother and friend and neighbor'." ²⁸The Levites did as Moses commanded, and that day about three thousand of the people died. ²⁹Then Moses said, "You have been set*

apart to the LORD *today, for you were against your own sons and brothers, and he has blessed you this day."*

³⁰The next day Moses said to the people, "You have committed a great sin. But now I will go up to the LORD; perhaps I can make atonement for your sin."

³¹So Moses went back to the LORD and said, "Oh, what a great sin these people have committed! They have made themselves gods of gold. ³²But now, please forgive their sin— but if not, then blot me out of the book you have written."

³³The LORD replied to Moses, "Whoever has sinned against me I will blot out of my book. ³⁴Now go, lead the people to the place I spoke of, and my angel will go before you. However, when the time comes for me to punish, I will punish them for their sin."

God had given Moses precise instructions to build a portable temple. It was very elaborate and complete with all the artifacts and furniture needed in their sacrifice-based worship of God. It was very elaborate; an outer wall made of cloth and posts, an inner *room,* the *Holy Place,* with furniture, and the inmost room, the *Most Holy Place,* with its insides hidden by a curtain. The Most Holy Place, the *Holy of Holies* hid the Ark of the Covenant and Aaron's staff which had sprouted, from sight. The Israelites had plundered Egypt, asking for every manner of valuables from them when they left. The Egyptians, glad to have rid of them, readily gave them what they asked for. They left with vast amounts of gold, silver, bronze, jewels of every type, and expensive cloths. The tabernacle would use some of everything; God planning again.

God was very specific about worship of Himself. There were no second warnings and stepping out of line got you zapped dead. God was very serious about His rules and even hundreds of years later a priest got zapped dead because he touched the Ark of the Covenant, which was most holy to God. The details about the portable temple are extensively detailed in Exodus, as are the laws and sacrifices in Leviticus.

God was having a hard time building a nation. Although numerically it had been a success, in their hearts, His new nation seemed to want to reject Him.

Now the old wine skins, the whiners, are at the border of the Promised Land, and as will become a repeating theme, God needs to refine His people, to sort those who trust Him completely from those who don't. He knows that the older generations will not be a good foundation to start the nation in the Promised Land, but He needs some concrete evidence of their lack of trust in Him to satisfy His justice. He needs a forward looking nation, not one that continually harps back to the *good old days* back in Egypt. It sounds rather callous, but He is going to condemn them to die off in the desert. His anger has raged against them already, and many have already died, and many more will die directly by His hand, but there are a few million of them that He needs to dispose of. They have shown a definite lack of respect and trust, even though He brought them out of Egypt with its treasure, kept

Pharaoh's great army from harming a single one of them, and kept them alive. Now He is going to present them with His plan for them directly. They are at the border of the Promised Land. They will not just whine but directly oppose God's plan.

Testing the people

The leaders of the people want Moses to send 12 spies, one from each tribe, to check out what is ahead in the Promised Land and Moses agrees; remember God knows what will happen. Only 2 of the 12 have a favourable report, the other 10 say "the land is occupied by giants," *the sky will fall on our heads*. What is God going to say, "Oh sorry, let me find a more acceptable land, a paradise with no one in it?" This is the last straw for God, the justification He needs to set them off for a forty year trek around the desert so that everyone age 20 and over will die off, everyone except Caleb and Joshua, the two spies with positive reports, and Moses, Aaron, and their families of course. God removes all of the older generations who are just too entrenched in the Egyptian culture, too inflexible for a change of this magnitude. Besides being too stubborn to accept that He would provide and protect them, being Sovereign He also required their obedience; they accepted dominance of the Egyptians, but could not bend the knee to God.

It gets worse, the Levites who maintain the tabernacle, the portable temple, openly rebel against God's chosen leaders, Moses and Aaron. God has shown Himself to the Israelites as clearly as the angels had seen Him in heaven. There is no doubting His existence or His intentions. It has nothing to do with keeping the law at this point; this is rebellion.

Numbers Chapter 16

¹Korah son of Izhar, the son of Kohath, the son of Levi, and certain Reubenites—Dathan and Abiram, sons of Eliab, and On son of Peleth—became insolent ²and rose up against Moses. With them were 250 Israelite men, well-known community leaders who had been appointed members of the council. ³They came as a group to oppose Moses and Aaron and said to them, "You have gone too far! The whole community is holy, every one of them, and the LORD is with them. Why then do you set yourselves above the LORD's assembly?"

⁴When Moses heard this, he fell facedown. ⁵Then he said to Korah and all his followers: "In the morning the LORD will show who belongs to him and who is holy, and he will have that person come near him. The man he chooses he will cause to come near him. ⁶You, Korah, and all your followers are to do this: Take censers ⁷and tomorrow put burning coals and incense in them before the LORD. The man the LORD chooses will be the one who is holy. You Levites have gone too far!"

⁸Moses also said to Korah, "Now listen, you Levites! ⁹Isn't it enough for you that the God of Israel has separated you from the rest of the Israelite community and brought you near himself to do the work at the LORD's tabernacle and to stand before the community and minister to them? ¹⁰He has brought you and all your fellow Levites near himself, but now you are trying to get the priesthood too. [11] It is against the LORD that you and all your followers have banded together. Who is Aaron that you should grumble against him?"

Can you imagine a nation, after seeing the power of God demonstrated for them, even parting the Red Sea so they could cross on dry land, having the arrogance to confront the obvious leaders that God had chosen; they get their answer.

Numbers Chapter 16

[16] Moses said to Korah, "You and all your followers are to appear before the LORD tomorrow—you and they and Aaron. [17] Each man is to take his censer and put incense in it—250 censers in all—and present it before the LORD. You and Aaron are to present your censers also." [18] So each of them took his censer, put burning coals and incense in it, and stood with Moses and Aaron at the entrance to the tent of meeting. [19] When Korah had gathered all his followers in opposition to them at the entrance to the tent of meeting, the glory of the LORD appeared to the entire assembly. [20] The LORD said to Moses and Aaron, [21] "Separate yourselves from this assembly so I can put an end to them at once."

[22] But Moses and Aaron fell face down and cried out, "O God, the God who gives breath to all living things, will you be angry with the entire assembly when only one man sins?"

[23] Then the LORD said to Moses, [24] "Say to the assembly, 'Move away from the tents of Korah, Dathan and Abiram'."

^{25}Moses got up and went to Dathan and Abiram, and the elders of Israel followed him. ^{26}He warned the assembly, "Move back from the tents of these wicked men! Do not touch anything belonging to them, or you will be swept away because of all their sins." ^{27}So they moved away from the tents of Korah, Dathan and Abiram. Dathan and Abiram had come out and were standing with their wives, children and little ones at the entrances to their tents.

^{28}Then Moses said, "This is how you will know that the LORD has sent me to do all these things and that it was not my idea: ^{29}If these men die a natural death and suffer the fate of all mankind, then the LORD has not sent me. ^{30}But if the LORD brings about something totally new, and the earth opens its mouth and swallows them, with everything that belongs to them, and they go down alive into the realm of the dead, then you will know that these men have treated the LORD with contempt."

^{31}As soon as he finished saying all this, the ground under them split apart ^{32}and the earth opened its mouth and swallowed them and their households, and all those associated with Korah, together with their possessions. ^{33}They went down alive into the realm of the dead, with everything they owned; the earth closed over them, and they perished and were gone from the community. ^{34}At their cries, all the Israelites around them fled, shouting, "The earth is going to swallow us too!"

³⁵And fire came out from the LORD and consumed the 250 men who were offering the incense.

I can't help seeing the technical elements at play here, even though God does not need help. To me it seems interesting that God often manipulates nature to fulfil His ends, such as blowing such a massive flock of meat and dumping on the Israelite camp to a depth of three feet. Note that the 250 dissenters are ordered to present their bronze censors, 250 lightning rods all grouped together. What do they get, lightning; each one of them burnt to a crisp. As a reminder God tells Moses to beat the censors into sheets and cover the altar with them.

40 years in the desert

The remaining few million Israelites wander around the desert for forty years, following the pillar of cloud, which moves them from place to place and stops for them to make camp. The pillar burns as fire at night. The spirit of God is in the pillar as a constant reminder. God provides manna, sweet tasting flakes that settle before dawn each day, except the Sabbath (Saturday), and turns mealy soon after dawn. From this they can make all sorts of breads etc. Their shoes and clothes do not wear out during the whole forty years. Was this a lesson or what; get with the program and trust in God, or pay the penalty?

There is much that I have skipped over in this brief recounting of the exodus of the Israelites from Egypt to the Promised Land. God threatened and maybe would have preferred to wipe out all the old wine skins, but deferred to Moses' compassion. God had a purpose, a plan. He wanted to move forward; dissenters were a hindrance. He had the old generation raise the new generation then die off. By the end they had the same number of people as when they started.

It was not just in the exodus but throughout the history of Israel that God has battled disobedience, not just of His commandments, but in the basic acknowledgement of His Sovereignty and Majesty.

The doorstep of the Promised Land

At the end of the forty years, God brought them to the Promised Land again. All the older generations had died off by this point and those originally under 20 (plus Caleb and Joshua etc.), had been well versed in God's Laws. Aaron had died earlier, and Moses saw, but did not enter the Promised Land. He handed the mantle of leadership to Joshua, his right hand man and one of the two spies who 40 years earlier had wanted to take the land. Moses reiterated the laws of God in a long and dramatic oration to the people before climbing a mountain to view the Promised Land then dying at the top and being taken to heaven by the Archangel Michael. Moses lived an astonishing life of enormous contrasts. He had an unfailing trust in God, and love for His nation. He lived 120 years, 40 years in Egypt, 40 years in Midian, and 40 years in the desert. His name is synonymous with servant.

Deuteronomy 34

¹Then Moses climbed Mount Nebo from the plains of Moab to the top of Pisgah, across from Jericho. There the LORD *showed him the whole land—from Gilead to Dan, ²all of Naphtali, the territory of Ephraim and Manasseh, all the land of Judah as far as the Mediterranean Sea, ³the Negev and the whole region from the Valley of Jericho, the City of Palms, as far as Zoar. ⁴Then the* LORD *said to him, "This is the land I promised on oath to Abraham, Isaac and Jacob when I said, 'I will give it to your descendants.' I have let you see it with your eyes, but you will not cross over into it."*

⁵And Moses the servant of the LORD *died there in Moab, as the* LORD *had said. ⁶He buried him in Moab, in the valley opposite Beth Peor, but to this day no one knows where his grave is. ⁷Moses was a hundred and twenty years old when he died, yet his eyes were not weak nor his strength gone. ⁸The Israelites grieved for Moses in the plains of Moab thirty days, until the time of weeping and mourning was over.*

⁹Now Joshua son of Nun was filled with the spirit of wisdom because Moses had laid his hands on him. So the Israelites listened to him and did what the LORD *had commanded Moses.*

Joshua

God urged the anointed Joshua "to be strong and courageous" three times in rapid succession. Obviously he and his flock face a daunting task ahead, daunting that is, for mankind. At this time the number of Israelites was about the same as when they had left Egypt; they still had just over 600,000 fighting men, but they were *less* than any of the seven nations in the Promised Lands that they had to conquer. Joshua prepared to cross the Jordan but agreed for the women, children, and flocks of 3 of the tribes to stay behind, as they wanted to settle there.

Joshua Chapter 1

[12] But to the Reubenites, the Gadites and the half-tribe of Manasseh, Joshua said, [13] "Remember the command that Moses the servant of the LORD gave you: 'The LORD your God is giving you rest and has granted you this land.' [14] Your wives, your children and your livestock may stay in the land that Moses gave you east of the Jordan, but all your fighting men, fully armed, must cross over ahead of your brothers. You are to help your brothers [15] until the LORD gives them rest, as he has done for you, and until they too have taken possession of the land that the LORD your God is giving them. After that, you may go back and occupy your own land, which Moses the servant of the LORD gave you east of the Jordan toward the sunrise."

The remainder crossed the Jordan, which was in flood stage, on dry land in another spectacular event. God promised them a huge swath of land. It was already just about fully occupied with feuding nations with detestable religious practices. He knew that just like the old wine skins from Egypt that could never be changed, they would have to go. The Israelites were not just outnumbered in total; they were outnumbered by each of the seven nations there. But they had a secret weapon that was not so secret. You don't annihilate Pharaoh's army and walk through the Red Sea on dry land without the word getting out. Even though they stayed in the desert, their Red Sea miracle experience lived on for 40 years. By the time they got to Jericho, the God of the Israelites' reputation had preceded them. The nations they faced had heard of the plagues on Egypt and the Red Sea crossing 40 years before, and what may have been turning into a myth was brought to sudden reality by the defeat of Sihon and Og, kings of the Amorites. Israelite spies entered Jericho to check it out.

Joshua Chapter 2

[8]Before the spies lay down for the night, she went up on the roof [9]and said to them, "I know that the LORD has given this land to you and that a great fear of you has fallen on us, so that all who live in this country are melting in fear because of you. [10]We have heard how the LORD dried up the water of the Red Sea for you when you came out of Egypt, and what you did to Sihon and Og, the two kings of the Amorites east of the Jordan, whom you completely destroyed. [11]When we heard of it, our hearts melted and everyone's courage failed because of you, for the LORD your God is God in heaven above and on the earth below.

In a mighty spectacle of power and sovereignty God demolished the immense fortress walls of Jericho in a way no one in Jericho, then or now could imagine. Although

600,000+ walking around the walled city, led by the Ark of the Covenant, must have been a logistical nightmare, it gave an update to their reputation as an invincible force. Unfortunately almost immediately pride and disobedience started to take its toll on God's plan. After Jericho was erased from the map, the Israelites suffered a humiliating defeat against the small town of Ai. God had told the Israelites they were not to keep anything from Jericho, the plunder was to go into the Lord's treasury; some was kept. God's punishment was swift, and a lesson to all that no one could hide anything from God.

In the many years that followed they were supposed to totally rid the Promised Land of the pagan people, who were evil in God's sight. Their practice of child sacrifice and deviant orgies were worse than Sodom and Gomorrah. They did this initially, killing everyone as they went from city to city, even as cities banded together to attack them. One city made a peace agreement. God specifically warned The Israelites not to do that. The city made out they were from far off, carrying moldy bread and wearing worn out sandals. They ended up being forced to be water bearers and wood cutters for the Israelites. The decision to make an agreement without consulting God came back to haunt them, probably continuing until the present day!

God wanted all trace of foreign gods, and the peoples who worshiped them in detestable ceremonies, removed from the land so the Israelites would not intermarry and be seduced by the pagan gods. God did not want people worshipping pagan idols in the presence of the Israelites luring them to follow the pagan Gods. But they did not totally remove the current inhabitants as God had told them, and consequently the plethora of pagan god worship remained and contaminated the Israelites in a phenomenal way throughout the whole time they occupied the Promised Land the first time.

Over the remainder of Joshua's lifetime, Joshua and the tribes of Israel replaced the inhabitants of many cities over a large area roughly the size of current Israel, but it was not all the land that God had promised. They completely replaced the inhabitants of the existing cities. Some decided to leave of their own accord, but after the initial ethnic cleansing as commanded by God; each tribe had its own designated land. The nation ended its combined occupation operations and each tribe was left to finish the job in their respective land. Most tribes never did finish the job and Israel spent most of its time warring with its neighbours as they do today.

Israel took over vacant cities, their flocks, their olive groves, their orchards, and their vineyards. Some ethnic groups were completely replaced by the various tribes of Israel, as if they had been there for centuries. As part of a long admonition, God spoke through Moses to the nation just as they were about to venture into the Promised Land.

Deuteronomy Chapter 6

[10]When the LORD your God brings you into the land he swore to your fathers, to Abraham, Isaac and Jacob, to give you—a land with large, flourishing cities you did not build,

¹¹houses filled with all kinds of good things you did not provide, wells you did not dig, and vineyards and olive groves you did not plant—then when you eat and are satisfied, ¹²be careful that you do not forget the LORD, who brought you out of Egypt, out of the land of slavery.

And in a long recounting of the path of the nation up to that time, Joshua spoke the Words of God to the whole nation at Shechem. He described the many miracles of God as they swept through the land, replacing many peoples who had developed and settled the Promised Land before them.

Joshua Chapter 24

¹³So I gave you a land on which you did not toil and cities you did not build; and you live in them and eat from vineyards and olive groves that you did not plant.

King David

Early on, despite their disobedience, King David conquered just about all the Promised Land, leaving a golden reign to his son Solomon, but after this God sifted them many times. He seems to have abandoned Israel, consisting of the northern tribes, who succumbed to intermarriage the most, and who's Kings led them, with great enthusiasm it seems, to worship foreign gods. They were eventually scattered by invading armies, leaving only the tribe of Judah and its succession of kings in a fraction of the southern region of the Promised Land. In a grand play, God used the Babylonians to even haul Judah off to Babylon for 70 years, having predicted the duration and even naming the Babylonian king who would let them return, through earlier prophets. He sifted them by letting those who wished, presumably those who trusted Him, to return. Only a fraction returned, and by this time the nation had been more than decimated to less than 10,000 people. In time God gave up trying to guide them with His prophets and they were (mis)guided by the elite Pharisees and Sadducees and a corrupt Governing legislature, the Sanhedrin. Skip some hundreds of years of God remaining silent and now they are subservient to the Romans, who were around their peak in domination of the known world. God had intended the Israelites to introduce their God to the rest of the world, but they developed an exclusive culture and utterly failed to do this. God had also proven conclusively that mankind could not keep a clear set of laws that would keep them holy.

Much of the Jewish life was centred on the temple, planned by David but built by Solomon, and the many sacrificial ceremonies conducted by the priesthood to atone for failure of the people to keep God's laws, individually and corporately.

Jesus

Jesus was born into a time where God's laws had been turned into a legalistic system of over 600 detailed rule-laws, making life drudgery for all except the pedantic Pharisees and Sadducees. Once a year there was a ceremony of atonement, where two goats were taken, one to be sacrificed, and the other on which the High Priest placed all the sins of the people and then cast it out into the desert, presumably to die. Jesus was God's answer for man's demonstrated failure to be holy, and was God's sacrificial lamb to atone for the sins of mankind for all time, replacing the sacrificial goats. Jesus predicted that He would rebuild the torn down temple in Jerusalem in three days. He did but not in chronological order; the Jewish Temple was destroyed after His resurrection. He built His temple, His church of Christian believers, when he was resurrected three days after being crucified, but it took another 37 years, in AD70, for the Jewish Temple to be torn down, along with Jerusalem, when the Romans put down the Jewish rebellion. They scattered the Jews, *and Christians*, all over the known world, successfully spreading Christianity far and wide. Jesus' Church had no need of animal sacrifices, but instead His Church was supposed to lead sacrificial lives, living as He did, caring for others. Because the Temple, the center of Jewish worship, was destroyed, the sacrificial system seems to have been destroyed with it, even though the scattered Jews had local temples all over the known world.

Age of Grace

What a plan, soon after Jesus crucifixion, at Pentecost, the Holy Spirit came to man as Jesus promised. The Church exploded, first in Jerusalem, then all over the Roman world via the fabulous Roman road system, under the relatively peaceful, even if it was oppressive, Pax Romana. The Church was so invasive and effective through the Holy Spirit that it was adopted, and somewhat corrupted, by the Roman Empire. The Church was no longer under the Law, the Mosaic Law, but under the Grace of God, through the blood of Jesus. Jesus had paid the penalty for all man's sins for all time, if they believed in what Jesus had done on the cross. Here we are today with the remnants of the Romans, who morphed the Church into a means of controlling the population, the Roman Catholic Church. The Protestant Church initiated by Martin Luther who rebelled against the corruption of the Roman Catholic Church in 1517, led the reformation back to the basics of faith in Jesus, over a 1,000 years later.

There is a pattern from the day they left Egypt, of God trying to sort and refine a people. He shows them His power, demonstrates His Sovereignty and Justice demanded by His Holiness, but the level of rebellion stands out even compared to the pagans. Today God's nation of Christians grows through the power of God and now stands around one third of Earth's population, growing most strongly in the most humble, and also as it happens, the most impoverished regions. As He did with the angels, God is separating His human creation, the sheep and the goats as He puts it. The day will come when the time of sorting and refining is over. There will be the sheep, those loyal and obedient to God, through the salvation work of Jesus, and God will take us home. Then there will be the goats, who are destined to be outside God's home where there is a *'weeping and gnashing of teeth'* as the Bible puts it. The earth will be pretty messed up by that time and God will press the reset button on the heavens and the cosmos.

God's plan to create a nation, Israel, *the apple of His eye*, was accomplished, and He gave the nation laws, temple rituals, feasts, and ways of living to prosper them. They could not live by the laws, as none of us can, but they could not even keep faith with Him, no matter how many times He would turn His back then return to save them from their predicaments. They did not present Him to the rest of the world. They perverted it into a highly exclusive and introverted legalistic system. Jesus came, not to abolish the law, but to give them a way to live in freedom from the law, out from under its condemnation because they could not keep it. The part of God's plan to show how powerless mankind was, had ended. The next part started, allowing mankind to live under Grace, where his sins were forgiven before they were even committed. They could live under Grace instead of the Law. Some Jews accepted this, but most did not.

God's gospel of Grace was taken to the Gentiles, non-Jews, by the apostles and the Jews who had accepted Jesus and His Grace. The Gentiles and the Jews who believed in Jesus and what He had accomplished, became His Church, the new Israel, His nation; the people later to be named *Christians*. According to the book of Romans, the remaining Jews will eventually come to accept Jesus as their Lord, so becoming a part of God's nation along with the earlier Jews. I think though, the book of Romans infers, that those who resist will wait until the time of tribulation to accept Jesus, but in the end He will bring His lost sheep into His fold to attend the Wedding Banquet with His complete Nation of Israel, His Church.

Dog Days

Like many Christians I have prayed all my Christian life for God to guide and direct my life. He has only done this clearly a few times and they were all connected to a time when I unequivocally gave my future to Him. Some years after I became a Christian I surrendered to Him, literally giving up my selfish ambitions, a very painful process. Back before the internet I wrote off for over 30 high-tech jobs from San Diego USA to Saint John's NL Canada. Fed up with the extreme ups and downs of my life to that point, I said to God that I would take the first offer regardless of salary. Three months later I was headed, I thought, to a job I didn't want, in a region of greater Toronto. Days before I expected the offer for this job, I received a call for the job I did want. I started the next Monday in British Columbia on the west coast of Canada and within a month headed up a department. It was a small company and unfortunately, after 3 months, the company imploded due to some extreme politics between the executive management and the board. My job was headed for the toilet. Strangely although this mimicked the extreme nature of my life, I was not worried, well, not after wrestling with the Holy Spirit for 3 hours. I said to God, "this may look like the consequences of one of my decisions, but it's not my problem it was Your plan, You have to fix it." Within a few days, after forming a new company with the executives who had all quit, I became a founding executive, with the accompanying founder's shares. Just before t the end of the dot com bubble I traded my shares for well over half a million dollars.

Now the earth was formless and empty, darkness was over the surface of the deep, and the Spirit of God was hovering over the waters.

~ Genesis 1:2

God's Weather Forecast

God sees the future; but how? Now just as a warning I have included supporting information for some statements in this Chapter. If it gets too technical just skip over that part, there is still plenty of meat to be had.

There are two ways to see the future. One is to wait for events to happen and then be able to either *see* into the future or to travel to that time personally or have someone do it for you and see directly what has or is transpiring. The other, is to set up all the influential parameters, that is set up the conditions, that will affect every detail, or the details that concern you, and let the future happen on its own, in a predictable way. Is your God capable enough to set the ball rolling at the beginning of creation with such predictability, even creating the "Big Bang" firework, but only needing to light the touch paper?

We're talking billions of years, of being able to extrapolate predictability so that He would be able to accurately *see* the future, what would seem to us to be billions of chance events billions of years into the future. That would involve knowing how every molecule would react with all the others to go through all the stages from the big bang to the current cosmos, and our cultures. Or maybe it would be enough to know that the earth would be formed, and safe from cosmic annihilation for the time span God needed it. Maybe God then *seeded* the earth with plants animals and mankind in sequence, and let mankind and every creature on the earth evolve within their species over eons by the same prediction method. Or did He let it develop in six stages, even stepping in to tweak it, like the asteroid landing in the Gulf of Mexico, causing a *nuclear winter* to wipe out the undesired dinosaurs. Or literally what the Bible says creating the cosmos, the whole earth, and everything in it, in six days. It doesn't really matter; I'm sure God could have done any of the above.

Predicting the choices of humans is not as impossible as it seems even for thousands of years, if you know the starting points and the influencing parameters, such as location, weather, and what all the other people are going to do and say. You just have to be really clever. In the short term we can make quite good assumptions, politicians do and say things to influence people, predicting that if you are in a particular demographic you will vote for them. Centuries ago in a study of human behavior predictions were delineated in the "Art of War." Ever thought exactly what God meant by the words in:

Romans Chapter 8

[29]*For those God foreknew he also predestined to be conformed to the image of his Son, that he might be the firstborn among many brothers and sisters.*

According to archeologists Homo sapiens, that's us, developed music and art over 35,000 years ago. An ivory flute and works of art were discovered in Germany recently and dated to around this time. In fact we appear to be just one of several variants of Homo erectus, just like there are many types of dog. Two other variations were around during the early times of Homo sapiens breaking out of Africa. The Neanderthals were not nearly clever enough to survive the ice age climate changes, but they left us a gene legacy that we benefit from before they went extinct. Another, Homo denisova, added huge natural immunity to the populations in South East Asia, when they interbred with Homo sapiens. These deductions are made by identifying DNA fragments originally found in the remains of those two extinct variations and comparing them to the DNA in specific races of modern man.

It doesn't matter which method or even which mix of methods caused our earth and us to come into existence. It is all temporary. God constructed a school for us to learn about Him. We successfully graduate when we have come to acknowledge Him. We take post graduate studies when we develop a relationship with Him, thus preparing us to eventually live with Him in whatever He creates after the existing heaven, earth and cosmos have passed away.

Revelation Chapter 21

[1]Then I saw a new heaven and a new earth, for the first heaven and the first earth had passed away...

Satan has schemes to manipulate the major events in this world, but never seems to get the outcome we assume he wants. He always appears to be one step behind, a bit like Wyllie Coyote. It would seem he cannot predict, or see the future, except what is allowed by his intellect. I don't think Satan can *see* because I don't think he has the power, but I have explained how an unlimited intellect can. Unfortunately for him, his intellect is limited. The more limited the intellect, the worse the accuracy of predictions.

We can also predict the future. Oh yes we can. Take an egg and hold it at waist height above a hard floor. Can you predict what will happen if you drop it? How about dropping it onto a carpet? How about from knee height? You can predict the outcome either by experience, or mathematically. The mathematical method is more accurate, especially when you feed all the variables about the strength of the shell when impacted at every angle, the weight of the egg, the energy absorbance of the floor, etc. If you fed every variable that affected the outcome into a sophisticated enough equation you could predict the outcome extremely accurately. This is a very simple example, but still very hard for mankind to do with precision. It's what we do with space rockets, with enormous effort and at great expense. It's why they can land on the moon and even land on asteroids. The world is bound by the laws of physics, and even God very rarely if ever, bends them.

When Jesus was being tempted to jump from the highest point of the temple in Jerusalem, Satan did not say, "…and

God will let you float down gently" (by reducing gravity significantly), but "… He would command angels to catch Jesus and let Him down gently."

Luke Chapter 4

9The devil led him to Jerusalem and had him stand on the highest point of the temple. "If you are the Son of God," he said, "throw yourself down from here. 10For it is written:" 'He will command his angels concerning you to guard you carefully; 11they will lift you up in their hands, so that you will not strike your foot against a stone'."

There are many statements about knowledge of things in the future such as:

Revelation Chapter 17

8…The inhabitants of the earth whose names have not been written in the book of life from the creation of the world…

I'm not talking about the prediction, but the statement about when the Book of Life was populated with names; it was before the earth existed. There are also many more detailed events that God claims to know about:

Matthew Chapter 10

29Are not two sparrows sold for a penny? Yet not one of them will fall to the ground apart from the will of your Father. 30And even the very hairs of your head are all numbered.

Hairs are a very dynamic asset for a man. They are there in our peacock days, but fall away in random numbers it seems, every day thereafter. How could you keep track of them for each of us! Is this a statement of metaphor, or was He *not* kidding! If you predicted every molecule, you could predict these things. How big is your God? He's bigger than even the most generous of us let Him be.

There is much we do not understand about the cosmos. Guiding a space craft to Mars, and having it land, deploy and roam around is peanuts compared to fully understanding everything in space itself. There are black holes, antimatter, and quarks to name a few enigmas. We have models of the cosmos starting with the big bang, but it's like comparing a finger painting to a masterpiece; we are as children at this. These models actually allowed us to predict antimatter, and then create it, and annihilate it by mixing it with matter. The whole thing was recorded as it happened in the massive Large Hadron Collider at CERN, the European Organization for Nuclear Research in Switzerland.

Mathematical models are basically complex equations that describe how things work, how they are defined. Working back from our present universe, which is expanding, astrophysicists have constructed mathematical models that show what happened from the moment of the theoretical big bang. Currently the ones we have about that are very basic, and *barely* describe how the cosmos developed. I am not saying the Bible's recounting of creation is wrong, but I hold that there is more to where we are now on earth and how it came into being, than the Bible story of creation tells us. We have a limited understanding of how to integrate the truth about what we see, an expanding universe, which points to it coming from a single point in space. Dinosaur bones, human bones and evidence of various states of technology, have been found in deposits, which seem to predate Abraham by tens of thousands of years; the Bible and all this is true at the same time. The Bible says that for the Lord, one day is as a thousand years and a thousand years is as a day. This I think is a very simple way for God to say "You are bound by simple and constant time, a basic element in all your equations of motion, but I am not." I know, I know, time changes depending how fast we are going, Einstein, but the reality is, ignoring travel at the speed of light etc., we all have the same time, and it goes by at the rate of 60 seconds every minute.

Our mathematical models of this earth and its weather systems, with data input from thousands of weather stations around and satellites above the world, predict our weather. Whoever has the best models and the fastest computers gets the best predictions. But we have only started to build our tower of Babel; our best models are far too simple and our best computers are far too slow, and they only provide a guide at best. We can see however, that with more data and faster, much, much faster computers, we could be much better.

Don't dismiss science, the expanding universe is real, we see stars that exploded millions of years ago, dispersing their matter to form new celestial bodies. When we view stars we can see a shift in the colour of their light, this is the Doppler Effect; the same as a train whistle changing tone when it passes by. As the light from an object goes away it drops in frequency; stars do the same with their light. When an object moves away from us, the light is shifted to the red end of the spectrum, as its wavelengths get longer. If an object moves closer, the light moves to the blue end of the spectrum and its wavelengths get shorter. From this we can calculate relative speed. When we do this with thousands of stars, we see that they are all moving away from a single point in space. Did they come from this point or did God set them in this specific motion on the fly just some thousands of years ago? On earth, dating articles by testing where the radioactive carbon that is in them is in its decay life is real, and can date carbon back to some tens of thousands of years.

The radiocarbon dating method is based on the fact that radiocarbon, $Carbon^{14}$, is constantly being created in the atmosphere by the interaction of cosmic rays with atmospheric nitrogen. The resulting radiocarbon combines with atmospheric oxygen to form radioactive carbon dioxide, which is incorporated into plants by photosynthesis; animals then acquire $Carbon^{14}$ by eating the plants. When the animals or plants die, they stop exchanging carbon with the environment, and from that point onwards, the amount of $Carbon^{14}$ they contain begins to reduce as the $Carbon^{14}$ undergoes radioactive decay. Measuring the amount of $Carbon^{14}$ in a sample from a dead plant or animal such as a piece of wood or a fragment of bone provides information that can be used to calculate when the animal or plant died. The older a sample is, the less Carbon[14] there is to be detected, and because the half-life of Carbon[14] (the period of time after which half of a given sample will have decayed) is about 5,730 years; the oldest dates that can be reliably measured by radiocarbon dating are around 50,000 years ago, although special preparation methods occasionally permit dating of older samples.

I am not saying we evolved from slime via monkeys, starting from completely lifeless water, soil and rocks, but as sure as two and two is four, there are many things we have discovered that biblical mankind could not have known. The point is it does not matter, there are many things which confounded our ancestors that confound us; belief in God and what Jesus did does not depend on it, but life is easier if we don't have to pick and choose what to believe when we read the Bible.

We have recognized from biblical times that we are relatively simple minded intellectually, compared to God, who created us and the cosmos, and probably most angels. Even so, we can also create stars in the night sky, spheres of twinkling blue, red, and green, with one carefully constructed firework. We have sent men to walk on the moon when our computers were not as smart as a modern thermostat. How capable do you think God is; how small a box do you keep God in? Could He set the cosmos in motion by carefully planning and constructing the biggest firework ever made; the Big Bang?

He could have planned the birth and death of every star. He would have known in advance every stage of expansion of the cosmos, from when it was just an unimaginable amount of energy one instant, to all the matter in the universe the next; compressed into the size of a pinhead, it would expand in the big bang, to what we see today. He could have planned the development of every nebula, every constellation, every star, every planet and moon. Did you know that even the level of oxygen in our atmosphere is perfect; too much and fires would never go out, too little and our bodies would not function too well.

Hebrews Chapter 11

³By faith we understand that the universe was formed at God's command, so that what is seen was not made out of what was visible.

Specifically it was made, created, by Jesus, and referring to Jesus, Paul said in his letter to the Colossians:

Colossians Chapter 1

¹⁵He is the image of the invisible God, the firstborn over all creation. ¹⁶For by him all things were created: things in heaven and on earth, visible and invisible, whether thrones or powers or rulers or authorities; all things were created by him and for him. ¹⁷He is before all things, and in him all things hold together.

From the equation $E=MC^2$, where E=Energy, M=mass, (how much something weighs), and C=speed of light, we get energy by converting matter to energy, as in the atom bomb, where some of the matter is converted into energy; the flash of light is part of the conversion process. By doing the reverse, matter is created, $M=E/C^2$, invisible energy divided by the speed of light squared becomes matter somehow. If you believe in the big bang, that's where the universe came from.

Our cosmos is orderly. Its order is sustained by Jesus, who created everything in our cosmos that was created, and in God's heavens, visible and invisible. He could have created it in days as we know them, or as He knows them. He could have created with a big bang, knowing exactly what the cosmos would be at the time you read this, or He could have tweaked it while it developed. I think tweaking is a cop out, and if He did it with a big bang, it worked perfectly. But life is another matter. Originally the earth was dead, ready for life, but dead. Everything had to appear in sequence otherwise it would have stalled. You can't have animals before you have plants; what would they eat? I believe God created all life, in its species, species do not breed with other species, or not successfully anyway; there are no reported cases of a fertile mule stallion (offspring of a horse and a donkey).

Life on earth is interesting; it is based on a double helix of DeoxyriboNucleic Acid or DNA for plants and creatures. They differ by their gene sequences. The complete genome, the total set of genes contained in the double helix for a plant is very extensive, it is incredibly extensive for a creature. An interesting point to understand is that by itself a buttercup will never mutate into an apple tree, let alone a fish. DNA is incredibly complex, and almost every occurrence of mutation cannot be replicated, although small changes in plants are possible, creating new species. Within a species, the genome may be simplified; like a black dog can have young of all colours, less colour equals less genes, but two white dogs cannot have anything but white pups, as they will have lost most if not all of the genes for colour. You cannot get more complex genomes, you only get simpler genomes.

Different species cannot procreate. Evolution requires genomes to become more complex, and even though this may be theoretically possible through mutation, slime could never remotely become human within the timeframes of even the longest estimates of evolution. All links between species have been shown to be fakes, no matter how much evolutionists wish them to be true. A dog cannot become an elephant, and a sunflower cannot become a maiden with golden hair. There are no fossil links between species; without this there is NO evolution, only intelligent creation, where God, Jesus alone created life; He breathed life into Adam. Homo sapiens were the only creatures capable of relationship with God; God brought mankind onto the scene when the world was ready. That was when the volcanoes had settled down, after the atmosphere could burn up meteorites, and after the atmosphere could support the lush forests to stabilize the atmosphere and make it suitable for creatures. A large meteor landed off the coast of Mexico, spewing so much dust and debris into the atmosphere that the sun was largely blocked out, causing what is called a nuclear winter for a number of years; a nuclear bomb has the same effect. The lush vegetation at least temporarily died off for a few years due to the lack of sunlight, and the larger mammals and dinosaurs that fed on them subsequently died out. Millions of years of lush vegetation became buried as mountains rose, forests sank below the water as the continents formed and shifted to create the world we know today. The vegetation rotted to peat and under heat and pressure later become oil, gas and coal. Maybe that was by day 6, maybe it was after 5 stages and billions of years.

 Dog Days

When I prayed to God for help to fix Jasmine's lack of intellect to comprehend training, my set of 10 commandments for dogs in my house, He said I was just like her. This made me start to check my nature; the way email is checked for spam and junk rules. I check myself for behaving like Jasmine. Far too often there is a positive correlation. My body has a lot more influence than I ever realized.

WE think we can train dogs, sometimes we can, sometimes we fail. According to dog whisperers, we are the problem, not the dogs. Who trains us? God had a set of rules. He tried to train His pet nation for thousands of years; He failed. But this time it was not the process, or the trainer, it was that the 'dog' had too big a brain; it was too proud and thought it was able to decide whether or not to follow its urges, not realizing that it was the urges that were in control.

After conclusively proving that fact, God revealed His new process, by giving us His Holy Spirit, who with our cooperation would renew our minds. Our renewed minds showed us that with God's help we could overcome our urges, and in times of weakness call upon Him for strength to not only overcome ourselves, our corrupted nature, but also outside influences, which have an intelligent, but malicious, plan for us.

You were blameless in your ways from the day you were created till wickedness was found in you.

~ Ezekiel 28:15

LUCIFER

Satan, mistakenly referred to as Lucifer or not, was created as an angel of the cherub class; he was anointed to be a *guardian cherub*, set to guard the Tree of the Knowledge of Good and Evil. In this book, because of tradition, he is referred to as Lucifer before his rebellion against God and Satan after. There is much evidence that the name Lucifer was a translational mistake in a Hebrew to Latin translation in the 4th century, that has been perpetuated in many translations ever since.

Ezekiel Chapter 28

^{12}"*Son of man, take up a lament concerning the king of Tyre and say to him: 'This is what the Sovereign* LORD *says:*

"'*You were the seal of perfection, full of wisdom and perfect in beauty.* ^{13}*You were in Eden, the garden of God; every precious stone adorned you: carnelian, chrysolite and emerald, topaz, onyx and jasper, lapis lazuli, turquoise and beryl. Your settings and mountings were made of gold; on the day you were created they were prepared.* ^{14}*You were anointed as a guardian cherub, for so I ordained you. You were on the holy mount of God; you walked among the fiery stones.* ^{15}*You were blameless in your ways from the day you were created till wickedness was found in you.* ^{16}*Through your widespread trade you were filled with violence, and you sinned. So I drove you in disgrace from the mount of God, and I expelled you, guardian cherub, from among the fiery stones. [17]Your heart became proud on account of your beauty, and you corrupted your wisdom because of your splendor. So I threw you to the earth;..."*

In this lament against Tyre, a wealthy and arrogant port city is compared to Lucifer, who is described in rich language. The statement in verse 15 infers that Lucifer had existed prior to being set as a guardian cherub over the Tree of Knowledge. "He was blameless in all His ways"; it takes time to develop a track record. A study of Lucifer will reveal that the name has to do with the brilliance of God's glory, and the conveyor of God's truth. He had a supreme intellect, and it could be reasoned he was to prepare mankind for God's truth, including the knowledge of good and evil. Pride was his downfall.

We should not be too quick to condemn Lucifer, in fact we should not condemn (judge) anyone; pride is one of our biggest problems as well. Pride in what we have, what we have accomplished, even pride in doing it our way, pride in regarding ourselves better than others. Our culture, or at least western culture teaches us it is good to be proud, proud of achievements, proud of our new bigger house, proud of our new car, the list goes on; the ongoing achievement of the *American dream*. Pride is only a few thoughts away from arrogance, and our culture quickly turns on us for taking pride too far, where pride becomes arrogance. But even then we have to go a long way into arrogance territory before that happens. Ask yourself how far you would get given all Satan's attributes. Is Superman too good to be true, aren't we more likely to be a Hancock (as in the movie), an arrogant and selfish version of Superman?

I think that was my problem when it came to surrendering to Jesus; I was driven, I had to succeed and I had to do it my way so I could take the credit for my success. Who doesn't try to be first to answer the Jeopardy question; why do we instinctively do that? Pride and arrogance are easy to see in others but hard to even notice in ourselves; this world makes it even harder as it lauds a good measure of it. Lucifer was aware of how gifted he was. Given free will he could see how enabling those gifts were, and how much more gifted he was over the other angels. In Isaiah 14:13 God says that Lucifer wanted to raise his throne above the stars, a reference to the other angels. There was only one problem; he was created by God to be His servant and had free will so he could do that in an intelligent and creative way, and develop a loving relationship with Him. I think free will forces us to make a decision; in time our true colours must show through. Apparently to exist as a servant, while being endowed with great gifts of power, intellect, and beauty created conflicts within Lucifer. Was he destined to rebel? Did God load him up with just too many superlative attributes that he would be unable to resist pride in every circumstance, eventually revealing a chink in his armour? Maybe the cards were stacked against him and he *was* destined to rebel. Jesus chose Judas, and he played a key role in triggering Jesus' crucifixion. Did Jesus know that when He chose him? Jesus had given up His Godly powers when He was born as a human. Did God feed Him selective knowledge; how soon was He aware of Judas' role?

After his downfall Satan is referred to as the dragon, or the beast. Why did he change, he didn't always rebel? Yes he was prone to be prideful, but pride needs something to feed on. Lucifer was at the top of his game, he was obviously elevated among the angels, and he was *brilliant* in more ways than one. He had gained a reputation of being blameless in all his ways. How long was it since he was created, thousands of years, millions, or even billions? There is no hint, and God has only inferred his existence before his appointment as guardian, or *covering* angel in His Bible. Maybe Lucifer had been given a job that he thought was not worthy of him. But whatever that was, it did not last; God was ready for the next phase of His plan.

God, through Jesus, created the cosmos and laid out his intentions for it, and the angel Lucifer's new role. Maybe he resented the attention God was paying to His new project, not the cosmos or earth, but humans, and His chosen people the children of Abraham. Lucifer goes from being a big fish in a big pond, to an isolated role ministering to those weak humans with spirits trapped in human *clay pots*. He must have seen us as far inferior, trapped in a realm of time and matter, visually oblivious to God's spiritual realm. The Bible refers to us as being *lower than the angels*, and even Jesus being like us and therefore also *lower than the angels* while

He was on earth. Maybe being the guardian cherub over the Tree of the Knowledge of Good and Evil in the Garden of Eden on earth, irked him. He was mighty among the angels; was he now relegated to take care of *God's people*, preparing them for God's truth, and eventually elevation above the angels? Would he do this work in isolation, bereft of acclaim; this work that needed the knowledge, wisdom, understanding, and strength, of a guardian cherub? Was it as simple as comparing himself with God, specifically Jesus, whom he seems to have had a particular beef with? Seeing little difference in his own eyes, is that what prompted him to become jealous, and prideful? Did he resent God giving the people of earth to Jesus?

John Chapter 10

[27] My sheep listen to my voice; I know them, and they follow me. [28] I give them eternal life, and they shall never perish; no one can snatch them out of my hand. [29] My Father, who has given them to me, is greater than all; no one can snatch them out of my Father's hand. [30] I and the Father are one."

Just as for us, his pride deluded him; he saw himself as equal to Jesus. Maybe he thought he was worthy of adoration by mankind and that *he* had earned it by his service to God in the past.

Whatever the seeds of discontent there was a turning point; instead of being a servant of God his Creator, Satan rebelled, effectively becoming an enemy of God. Now he set his own course of ultimate failure, disgrace, and banishment. Did

God foresee this? I believe He did. But then comes the inevitable question of why would He appoint Lucifer to the essential position guardian cherub of the Tree of Knowledge? Instead of protecting the Tree of Knowledge of Good and Evil, and preparing men to understand God's truth and light, he simply dumps it on them, totally unprepared, a total inversion of his role. Was this part of God's plan; if God is all knowing and all seeing, it had to be?

In order to maintain a relationship a person needs to interact deeply at the character level. Some creatures mate for life; mates being chosen on hardwired demonstrations of procreation ability. Often this is somehow conveyed in how much of a *peacock* they are and how well they can dance; oh wait, isn't that the way humans do it? In humans however evidence of real relationship is endurance, really becoming one. 50% of marriages fail to endure, and some endure out of convenience or fear. Do humans have a greater degree of free will than animals have; do we require knowledge about good and evil, a sense for it, an understanding of it, to assess character.

We were made in the image of God; we do not need the commandments to know murder is wrong. Animals do not in general murder. They may kill for many instinctive, hard wired, response to circumstance, reasons, but they do not murder; even though, you could argue their actions mimic us in similar circumstances. If they do murder, the Bible says they will be held to account for the blood they spill. Angels rebelled against God; angels are not hard wired. Some chose

God without wavering, some followed Satan quickly; others wavered and needed convincing. They had free will and chose by way of reason, even though their reasoning was most likely based on lies. If God let angels choose to separate into the loyal and the disloyal, why wouldn't He do the same with us? The same; the angels by default were all *with* God; they were separated by leaving God. The Bible says that when Adam and Eve partook of fruit of the Tree of Knowledge of Good and Evil, offered by Satan, we were all corrupted, fallen; we were all *with* Satan. We are separated by leaving Satan and choosing God. For God to separate us, drawing us to Himself from Satan, wouldn't we need to understand the difference between good and evil? We know we instinctively have the knowledge of the difference between good and evil; was it part of God's plan?

Someone recently asked me "What is evil?" What seems a simple question is not simple but extremely profound. I side stepped it somewhat by answering "Anything that goes against God's commands." That simplistic answer infers that God only commands good ways for us, and His standard is absolute. It also infers we are subservient to Him, deferring to His absolute definitions of good ways. To think anything else is rebellion against Him, at least from His perspective as our Creator; and therein lies the rub. We have an inbuilt paranoia about robots and GMO's (Genetically Modified Organisms); will our creations behave the way we intended them to; should we have a set of commandments for them? Should we have any compassion for a robot not obeying us as it explored its free will, or would we summarily nuke it? What do we do with a dog that bites a child? We are so self-righteous in our arrogance. Yes the dog needs to be put down as it is a danger to our children, but dogs do not know our *commandments*. It's the way we have bred it to be; its training and or circumstances drove it to bite. Dogs learn behavior, even to read our mood by studying the right side of our face, in order to derive the most pleasant existence they can; they do not agree to live by our *commandments*.

Did God have multiple reasons, like plots in a Shakespeare play, when He placed Lucifer as guardian of the Tree of Knowledge of Good and Evil? Was it the trigger for Lucifer to reveal his latent pride *and* to bring mankind into the awareness needed to actually choose to obey God or to reject His sovereignty; to go our own way? Awareness the angels already appeared to have, along with a nature that could embrace rebelling against God. Without that knowledge, that awareness, would we be His pet dogs? The Bible says that we demonstrate love for God through obedience; it is a choice, not a conditioned behavior.

1 John Chapter 5

²This is how we know that we love the children of God: by loving God and carrying out his commands. ³This is love for God: to obey his commands. And his commands are not burdensome.

"...I tell you, there is rejoicing in the presence of the angels of God over one sinner who repents."

~ Luke 15:10

ANGEL SOCIETY

Keeping the notion that God is all seeing, all knowing, and has all power in mind, when God created everything, it was not all at once. Even without getting into creation vs. evolution, the angels and other heavenly beings were created before the earth. So God, Jesus to be correct, created the angels. Why? Couldn't He do anything He wanted; create with just a thought that Jesus would translate into form? Why did He need angels? Maybe He was lonely? Not. Most likely He created them for some of the same reasons He created mankind, for His pleasure, and to serve and worship Him.

There is a hierarchy in God's heaven, there is order not chaos. As we see in the cosmos, there is order. There are laws of physics going far beyond Newton's laws of motion. There is anti-matter and dark matter; the mystery seems endless. We even arrogantly named the tiny Higgs boson particle after God; we called it the *God particle*. There are equations involving gravity twisting our cosmos and bending light and a direct relationship between matter and energy, in Einstein's $E=MC^2$. The cosmos is an unbelievably complex place. It goes far beyond the simple models of the planets revolving around the sun of our solar system and Newton's laws of motion; laws that describe not only the obvious orbits, but also every miniscule variation of tilt and wobble.

The mathematics of the cosmos seems a bottomless pit of research. But for God, was it as simple as God exchanging some of His infinite power, in the form of energy, for matter, to create the cosmos. Whether a big bang and six stages of evolution or simply six literal days of *spoken into existence creation*, it had to come from somewhere.

But we are talking of angels, in their realm of God's heavens. It all comes back to free will. It is clear from Lucifer's degeneration to Satan, at the beginning of human awareness of good and evil, that the angels, including Lucifer, existed before us and the earth. They had free will; they had society! They talked amongst themselves. What is free will if it cannot contemplate its options? The mere existence of free will exposed the angelic society to the opportunity to explore its options.

Their options do not include sexual lust, as they are spirits in God's heavens and incapable of intercourse. God's heaven likely includes time, space, and matter in some form or the prophets' visions of heaven were purely a mind game. God created as many angels as He wanted, they did not need to procreate. Besides, all the angel names we know are male names; there is no reference anywhere to female angels. They are powerful and beautiful yes, but there are no females. They are manifested on earth, and in heaven, in the form of males. Maybe they were males on earth in biblical times because of the patriarchal societies. Regardless they are not females, not the soft, gentle, images pictured in art over the last few hundred years. To a large extent, powerful, scary angels have been morphed into harmless, singing angels, by their inevitable commercialization. The three angels visiting Abraham, prior to obliterating Sodom and Gomorrah, are referred to as men, but Abraham still fell on his face. In heaven, visiting humans either faint or quake, but all fall on their face; they don't stare at their beauty with dropped jaws. They obviously have an aura of power and authority.

Hebrews Chapter 1

[14]Are not all angels ministering spirits sent to serve those who will inherit salvation?

It is clear in this verse that the angels were created to minister to humans, even though they were created more powerful than humans. Simply put, angels were created to be servants of God ministering to His other creation, mankind. This verse is interesting in that it does not define those *who will inherit salvation*. Its scope could be greater than humans; we are in the scope but may not comprise the full scope. Could there have been previous civilizations, like humans but not of our earth, but of whom there is no mention in the Bible; could there be others in the future? There are other creatures mentioned in the Bible, but not many, it does not infer they have numbers comparable to humans or angels. The reason I bring this up is that it would seem to have been possibly a long period of time before Satan was set to guard the Tree of Knowledge; he had garnered a reputation; he was found *blameless*. What had happened during this period; were their others that the angels ministered to?

This verse is part of the letter to the *Hebrews*, the Israelites, by someone, who many consider to be Paul, using words that were inspired by God, but the book is not written in Paul's usual style. There is also the statement in 1 Colossians Chapter 6 verse 3, where it refers to the children of God, us, judging angels. Now angels here, refers to 'good angels' as in the original text it is unqualified, no reference to them being fallen. These are the ones who did not rebel against God. Just because they did not rebel, were they perfect? Lucifer is referred to as being blameless in all his ways. If all angels were blameless this would not have been stated regarding Satan. Presumably angels were capable of making mistakes, shirking their duties, or even doing something other than what they were sent to do because they thought they knew better. On the other hand, because God is Holy, He cannot have sin in His presence. Is being less than perfect a sin? Even though I believe that everyone in God's presence must be holy, in Job God conversed with Satan. Could he have done this in His presence, can God tolerate unholiness in His presence? Why did God turn away from Jesus, after He placed the sins of mankind on Jesus, when Jesus was on the cross? The Bible says Jesus became sin.

The fate of the angels who rebelled with Satan is sealed and in God's hands, as expressly iterated in the Book of Revelation. It seems those who have errantly elevated themselves above their station or sought an existence other than under the sovereignty of God have also separated themselves from God. Unfortunately that comes under the umbrella of rebellion, and as they rejected their maker it is about as serious as it gets. It's much worse for them than it is for us; angels were created with knowledge of and *existed with God*, not that their fate will be different, but it seems that the degree of punishment may be different. We humans have no choice but to grow into rebellion as is our nature. We are born corrupted, *separated from God at birth*, and without a way to correct it by our own ability. Jesus created a way, salvation, where He covers that rebellion by His righteousness, but we have to want it, to seek to be made right with God. As for all rebellion, though, there are serious consequences. Trying to avoid the consequences by trying to explain away the reality created by God, is just wishful thinking. God is bound by His own justice.

As reasoned in the Chapter *If I was God*, true love is only capable of existing with free will, and the options to exercise it. Free will in an extreme dictatorship is not free will, as the options are 'bad, worse, terrible, and death'. That is not free will that is an existence controlled like livestock.

God is Love. We can't fully understand that. He created us, and presumably the angels, for His pleasure which includes a relationship. He wants a loving, caring, respectful relationship between us, His angels, and Himself. Without getting into the theology, we as humans are reconciled to God the Father, by the blood of Jesus, that is, the crucifixion of Jesus, and by Jesus accepting the penalty required by our sins at that time, but only if we believe that Jesus could and actually did that for us. *Thus there is only one name, Jesus, through which mankind may come to the father.* Angels are, or were, in direct contact with God, we are not; a different standard applies. We are all servants of God, at this stage in God's plan. Angels minister to us, and we minister to each other, but we have to believe and serve Him whom we do not see.

Angels may not be subject to sexual lust, but all the other lusts still apply to angels; the desire for power and control, pleasure, self-determination among others, with their accompanying behavior such as lying, deceit, anger, and rage. Angels may have existed for millennia, but all it took was for a leader, like Lucifer, to foment unrest; war in heaven was inevitable.

This describes our human society, but this was heaven. The angels were created by God, and they were quite aware of it. They could see Him! But still the characteristics of free will emerged. Resentment in some, had probably been manifesting itself as irritation or restlessness for a long time, for others it may have been quite latent; they may not have even been conscious of it until Satan showed his colours and stirred the pot in the society of angels.

"What no eye has seen, what no ear has heard, and what no human mind has conceived" the things God has prepared for those who love him.

~ 1 Corinthians 2:9

The Banquet

I leave you with these last thoughts that came to me one night as I lay awake in bed. They were about our wedding banquet with Jesus, the Lamb, and Author of our salvation.

In the blink of an eye I was in a huge amphitheatre, a massive space the size of a small city. The gigantic curved slopes were terraced with deep steps, and with hundreds of millions of tables of various sizes set along the steps. The tables were large enough for twelve or more to sit at with everyone being able to face the centre. God sits in the centre on an impressive throne made of solid sapphire with inset jewels. The throne had six steps, there was a footstool of gold; Jesus stood at God's right hand. Both glow in regal splendour, almost as if on fire, and illuminate the whole amphitheatre, which is made of almost transparent quartz. The Father holds a sceptre made of a single brilliant amethyst crystal with gold bands; it radiates a brilliant purple light. The centre of the amphitheatre is bathed in rich blue light from of the throne of God. On the first step are the Elders, Prophets, and the faithful Kings of His nation Israel. On the next layers of steps I see those who must the 12 tribes of Jacob, as there are 12 slightly separated groups of thousands.

The faithful in Christ, both angels and saints, are gathered around the tables on the steps reaching up many levels. We are gathered with family, reunited. Friends with their families are gathered around neighbouring tables. So many friends we know, and so many, many more we have yet to meet, eventually the billions will be as close family.

Light shines from everywhere, the brilliant white linen robes of the saints shine with the righteousness of Jesus. The saints do not resemble their male or female human selves; like the angels, they have beautiful faces reflecting their character, neither male nor female, as there is no differentiation of glorified bodies. Old, worn out bodies, ravaged by time or struggles, have been transformed into perfect bodies, like athletes, with unblemished skin that does not need adornment, except for hair, which represents the saints' hearts, in colour and style. An angel accompanies every saint. "Is that King David I see" I ask my angel, "and there, that must be Moses?" Every saint is asking questions as fast as they can speak.

The tables, made of crystallite, have fine threads of gold and glittering silver running through them. Rubies, sapphires, topaz, and emeralds, and other beautiful gems, from the size of grape seeds to the size of olives, are embedded inside the crystallite to form all manner of brilliant flowers. The tables are set with the most delicious wines with bowls made of single carved pearls full of fruits from the Tree of Life. The wine is the finest ever made, it warms the heart, but does not intoxicate, and the strange fruit seems to almost change in appearance while I watch it. Every saint gasps at their first taste, tasting more wonderful than food ever tasted, and the

The Banquet

wines are so smooth and invigorating, lifting our spirits higher, if that were even possible.

The Father is so bright it is hard to distinguish His features; He shines with His Love. All the saints look to be in their youth or prime, between 15 and 30 years old. The saints have their new immortal, glorified bodies, individual, but perfect, all wearing brilliant white robes of the softest linen. Their apparent age is a testimony to their maturity in Christ.

The attending angels are also dressed in shining white robes; they have silver waist sashes, like cummerbunds, with insignia embroidered on them in gold with fine jewels, which tell of their class, office, and past deeds. The angels are easy to pick out in the crowd; they are between 8 and 9 feet tall, with different builds, but all have a marvellously impressive stature. This must be their natural state in heaven, the way they appeared to the few humans who visited heaven in the Bible stories I read. Some have wild, fire-red, long hair; others, slightly smaller, have wavy golden hair, the colour of gold refined by their exploits. As with us, their hair reflects their hearts.

There are a number of angels with a stoic stance, arms folded but grinning, in the centre and standing some distance behind the throne. A presentation ceremony is about to start, great rejoicing erupts, spontaneous bursts of singing of new songs; angels singing the most complex layered harmonies, praising the Lamb, and giving glory to the Father. The attending angels usher the older looking saints down the deep steps to the centre. They are led down the broad steps and form a huge huddle of millions in the area in front of the centre. The Father stands, and the whole amphitheatre hushes and bows low.

The Father's arms rise as if to hug the whole congregation. He speaks; His voice is like a thousand voices speaking in perfect unison, with a tone of utter peace and joy, "Welcome everyone to the wedding feast of My Son. Like you My children, I have waited a long time to hear those words," and looking to the huddle before Him, He continues "Welcome good and faithful servants, come and receive your reward." Angels hand Jesus embroidered waist sashes of gleaming silver embroidered with crowns of gold. Combinations of jewels are embroidered into the gold crowns, which tell of the history of the saint and the crowns. One by one the saints are led up the steps to Jesus. "Welcome faithful friend." In one fluid motion He fastens the sash around the waist of the saint and kisses them.

Even though the presentation lasts a long, long time, the revelry does not die off. As the sashes are presented the crowns tell the story of that saint amid cheers of hallelujah, and choruses of "Holy is the Lamb." Even though there are hundreds upon hundreds of millions of saints and many more angels, all can see and hear the Father and Jesus, and the presentations, as if they are just across the table. There is time and space, but it is different, distance is where your mind is, not your body. Everyone is standing, and every now and then the whole congregation bows down with their faces to the ground, worshipping God, while the saints join the angels in the new songs, gradually learning the harmonies. The angels, who rejoiced in heaven, as each of us bent the knee to God on earth, now cheer, rejoice as if to burst, as all their efforts over the millenniums blossom as a flower that has been biding its time through a long and difficult spring.

When the presentations are complete, a mighty angel steps forward, turns to face God and bows with his face to the ground; everyone bows low. The Father, beckons with His hand, "Rise Michael, faithful warrior of my Word." Slowly the archangel rises and turns to the silenced congregation. As he raises his right hand a gleaming broad sword appears in it; he raises it high. On it is written 'True and faithful Words of God'. "Faithful friends and brother angels, let me tell you of the new heaven and new earth, which is to come." His voice is as mighty as his stature and it is as if the words he speaks are carved in stone. He foretells of the coming restored earth, with a New Jerusalem, and of the new nations who will inhabit the earth. He lowers the sword and it vanishes. Another angel steps forward, as Michael returns to his post behind the throne. He turns as Michael did and bows with his face to the ground. The congregation bows low and the whole amphitheatre is so silent you can hear the angel breathing. God lifts His upturned hand, "Rise Gabriel, faithful messenger of my Word." Gabriel stands and turns to face the congregation, his hand rises and the same sword appears in it; he holds it high. The words 'True and faithful Words of God' on the sword seem alive, as if they are the

Holy Spirit in person. "You are priests of the one and only God; Jesus is your high priest. You will govern and teach the nations the true Words of God, so they will walk in His ways and there will be peace and love in God's new heaven and new earth. He will be their God and they will be His people, and they will know each other in love." Gabriel lowers his arm and retraces his steps.

Jesus lifts His arms; everyone bows low. "Welcome home faithful friends. Now you see the face of your God, who was once hidden in your times of trial, but now God your Father will be the light of your life forever. This is our banquet, enjoy it with me. There is time enough." Jesus walks down from the centre, and then up the terraced steps and embraces every saint, one at a time; He chats, there is no hurry.

The saints and angels sit, we are all brothers and all have their stories of glorifying God with their lives. No one is hurried, it is the wedding reception, and it could have lasted a thousand years, as is a day in the realm of God. Jesus is always close, He is approachable, and never gets tired of the expressions of wonder and thanks offered by the saints. He seems always available to all at the same time, there are no line ups. Every now and then wonderful songs of praise erupt from a distant part of the amphitheater, and conversations come to a temporary halt as the praise migrates like a wave and the billions in attendance submit to it. Holy waves of the most beautiful singing wash over and over; it is if the air itself is alive with praise and love.

The Banquet

After what already seems like an eternity to the saints, beautiful angels pair off with those saints whose hearts, although faithful, are in tatters from their struggles on earth; they go off to be healed by the waters of the river of life, and the healing leaves of the trees besides the river. Some go off for instruction by the angels, to mature, regarding the ways of God, and others go for training from the messenger angels regarding their role of priesthood and teachers for the new nations.

There is time and space and our bodies are real, but it is not the same as it was before. Ages seemed to have passed, years and years, but we never tired, we never slept. The banquet is over, but it seems like the elation and joy in our hearts will last forever as we go our ways. The Bible was so right; we could never have imagined the fullness of the joy and peace, the feeling of being home, and the all-embracing love of our Father, His Son Jesus, all the other saints, and the angels.

But seek first his kingdom and his righteousness, and all these things will be given to you as well.

~ Matthew 6:33

My Testimony

I find it very interesting to hear how people encountered God for the first time and why they made the decision for Jesus to be the Lord of their lives. Here is mine.

Even though I had not come from a church going family I had a good childhood. The seeds of my relationship with God were planted during the few years I attended a Sunday school between the ages of five and nine. Even then, and even though I had not grasped the essence of Jesus, I felt I had a relationship with God.

He tugged at me through the years, and at the age of 30 I started to attend church. After 10 years, I heard the salvation message; I sat horrified in the pew, realizing that I was not saved and could have died many, many times already. I hurriedly gave my life to Jesus. That did it! Those few, simple words, muttered in haste, opened the door to Jesus; and boy did He come in. We found a new church that would not take ten years to preach the good news of salvation. I felt at home immediately in that new church. On the second Sunday, having no time for chit chat, I beat a hasty retreat to the exit once the service was over. This was the turning point in my life.

God spoke to me as I grasped the doorknob....

Later I worked out it was Jesus who spoke to me. He spoke audibly at first, "David", I could tell from the direction of the voice He was behind me, over my right shoulder, nine feet high. I spun around. There was no one there.

But He was there.

"Whose life is it?" He asked calmly. "Yours Lord" I answered feeling quite smug about my quick and confident response, after all I was only a two week old Christian. Then came the few simple words that rocked me to my core....

"So what are you going to do about it?" God has a way of making sure you know what He means. A question with so many possible answers, to me begged only one.

What could I say? I had oh so innocently spoken the words only two weeks before and asked Jesus to be the Lord of my life. There I stood before God. It was clear that I was as transparent as glass to Him. I could not side step the question; I could not smooth talk my way out of it. I could not retreat; I had said the words, the words I really did want to say, words I believed, but until that point, did not fully comprehend. I understood at that moment that it really was His life. The things on my list that I wanted to do, the things that would take four or five lifetimes to complete, were instantly paraded before me in my mind; it was one of those moments when your life flashes before your eyes. I knew Jesus wanted me to let go of it, all of it. To let my lists blow away in the wind, to let the pictures of my ambitions dissolve like vapour into the air. I gave it up.

It wasn't quite as simple as that. I went kicking and screaming. But when the dust settled, I had no list. As I started down the other fork in the road, I had just vague memories of my previous ambitions. I expected God to give me pictures and a list for my new life in Him, although He never said He would. As God had actually spoken to me, I thought He might have something special He wanted me to do. I thought I might be special. I was; I was Special Ed. Years later, I realized that I was so self-focussed that speaking to me was probably the only way He was going to get through to me. Even though it was an event of a lifetime, looking back in reality, it was more like being caught by the principal skipping out of school and having him drop a few words of reality in your ear.

Now 25 years later, I ponder those wasted years, my head still buzzing with my latest, but unfinished, life consuming technical marvel, while I struggle to make it let go of me so I can finish this book. I looked all those years for signs that God had a Kingdom job for me. He gave me great secular jobs, a wide variety of great houses to live in, even a number of great cars, but no Kingdom jobs, not the type I was looking for anyway. Maybe those years were not wasted; I am not the first person, who, wanting to do God's work was sent off into some backwater so they could be made ready. I think of Moses, Paul, and many others.

For all my praying and thinking that I was making myself available, my head was just buzzing with technology ideas, or was it that my *old man* was not dead. I kept taking on careers and jobs to put bread on the table for sure, but I'm also sure, looking back, I took jobs I could not resist because technology was a kind of god for me. However, I know God gave me my last technology job, one that I did not know existed. I got a job offer based on a one liner in my online resume. It was a job doing the technical write-ups for tax refunds based on research and development costs that companies incur. This was a commission based job and was quite lucrative, and it allowed me to spend most of my time developing the next technological widget that the world needed so desperately.

After four years maybe God thought I had been lying in the desert sun of Midian long enough and was fully baked; He took the job away. Being a bit slow on the uptake, and with my head buried in my best project since sliced bread, besides my paying job, it took me over a year to realize my bread and butter job was over. My commission income had dried up due to the Canadian Revenue Agency getting a new hair style; it was a bad hair day for me and I was next to broke. I tried desperately to get a job; I am not a web programmer, where most of the jobs seemed to be, but well-qualified for a wide range of engineering jobs. There seemed no shortage of jobs, and I'm sure there were not too many people with my 40+ years of diverse experience looking for them. Nada. Nada. Nada. I prayed, nada.

Now, months later, having had time to do a lot of research and reading, I realize that I was probably waiting for a Kingdom job that suited my talents, rather than the spiritual gifts that God would give me to do a job that He wanted to do through me. The significant word there is *through*. I wanted to use my talents and have been trying to find a way for 25 years to use my talents for Kingdom work. My last uncompleted plan was to provide jobs by starting an understanding company for people who had completed drug and alcohol rehabilitation, but were still not ready to enter the mainstream.

It was a big, bold, plan. I had all the execs, managers, and counsellors lined up waiting to go. We would make millions, hundreds of millions, for the investors and pay for the "bridge from rehab" program. I had developed a plethora of technical products to supplement and support the series of completely silent electric outboard motors from up to 100 horsepower. For over a year, thinking that this was God's next plan for me, I pursued the $8M that was needed to get the big idea off the ground. I was delayed and stymied at every turn. In the end, totally broke, I was still planning mini versions of the product line, but now just wanting to support myself. Very disillusioned with my local venture capital broker, for the first time in my life my enthusiasm for technology started to die.

A number of years before, when I'd had the idea for this book, my big, bold plan for the company was just a seedling. Now, that business having failed to blossom, the desire of getting back to that book started to grow within me again. Having bridged the years from when my job faded to this time of transition, with much help from friends and pensions from previous lives that started to kick in, we are able to survive. Now in modest housing that we would not have considered before, but with good neighbours, good views and perfect quiet, God has given me a job that I hope has Kingdom implications. I have no stress, and love this new lifestyle. I don't know where the ideas that I brain dump into this book come from, they just pop into my head at the oddest times. Just this morning clarification came for a number of jumbled ideas about the war in heaven, which I will now add to that Chapter.

The take away from all this: Kingdom jobs, distinct from living the Christian life of a servant, are where God works through you with spiritual gifts that enable you to do those jobs, mostly having nothing to do with your ongoing talents. I heard recently that if non-Christians took spiritual gifts test, they would come up with a list of gifts, that, as they were non-Christians, we would call talents. If they then became Christians and retook the test, they would get the same results, but we would call them spiritual gifts. Obviously they are not; they are talents. It seems that God gives us spiritual gifts to work through us. I know of a young man who went to South America on a mission trip. When he woke up on the first morning, he found he was fluent in Spanish; now that's a spiritual gift! A similar thing happened to a fellow from my church on a mission trip to India. He was crossing a bridge into a particularly demon-oppressed city in India. He could speak very little Hindi, but when he engaged a local man in conversation, all of a sudden he was perfectly fluent; when he went on his way the gift left him.

I have been trying to make sense of my life since I became a Christian, trying to discover God's plan for my life. I have seen His fingerprints sometimes, like cat footprints walking across the hood of your car; they show where He has been guiding, but I've never been able to see the path ahead. Even Moses didn't seem to get that. God told him to go to Pharaoh and perform miracles until he released the Israelites, but He didn't tell him what would happen after. Not until they were at a transition point did God layout the next stage; even the 40 years wandering in the desert was done in stages of following the Pillar of Cloud in the day and the Pillar of Fire at night. When it moved they followed; when it stopped they camped. For most of my Christian life, I didn't get that.

About the Author

DAVE SHAW has migrated from being a reluctant technical author to an enthusiastic author of Bible related books. A 25 year period of Bible study, paralleled the last half of a 50 year hands-on technology career, mainly as an intense designer. Now he's using his highly analytical mind to answer many of the 'whys' he's encountered while studying the Bible. Dave doesn't take credit for the answers, as they 'just come', and as he has diligently prayed about them, hopes in all sincerity they are inspired. When he's not writing, you can often find him staring into space. He says he's contemplating; his wife is not so sure.

Connect with Dave Shaw

I really appreciate you reading my book! I would love to hear your feedback. Being an engineer by training, I had my social media genes removed during training, but you can still contact me with your own 'why' list, and read my blog via my website, http://www.DaveShawAuthor.com, or on my Smashwords page at:

https://www.smashwords.com/profile/view/daveshaw13

You can dialog with me and others on my Facebook book page at:

https://www.facebook.com/profile.php?id=100009372179235 or email me at dave@daveshawauthor.com.

Made in the USA
Charleston, SC
05 July 2015